A CREATIVE STEP-BY-STEP GUIDE TO

THE
COTTAGE
GARDEN

A CREATIVE STEP-BY-STEP GUIDE TO

THE
COTTAGE
GARDEN

Author
Ann James

Photographer
Neil Sutherland

AURA

4399
This edition published in 1998 by Aura Books
Copyright © 1996 Quadrillion Publishing Ltd.,
Godalming Business Centre, Woolsack Way,
Godalming, Surrey, England. GU7 1XW
All rights reserved
Printed and bound in Singapore
ISBN 0-94779-301-1

Credits
Edited and designed: Ideas into Print
Photographs: Neil Sutherland
Typesetting: Ideas into Print and Ash Setting and Printing
Production Director: Gerald Hughes
Production: Ruth Arthur, Sally Connolly, Neil Randles,
Karen Staff, Jonathan Tickner

THE AUTHOR

Ann James' love of plants was kindled at the age of three
by the passionate enthusiasm of an aunt who insisted that
she look - really look - at flowers and their setting.
Theatre training at the Birmingham Repertory Theatre
focused her awareness of 'setting the scene' in the garden
as a natural extension of the interior design she was
engaged in with her husband after their seven children left
home. Over the past 20 years, designing and building
gardens has become the major part of their work, Robert
as garden architect and Ann specializing in planting design
and presentation. Their own cottage garden at 'The
Thumbit' has been featured in leading publications.

THE PHOTOGRAPHER

Neil Sutherland has more than 25 years experience in a
wide range of photographic fields, including still-life,
portraiture, reportage, natural history, cookery, landscape
and travel. His work has been published in countless
books and magazines throughout the world.

Half-title page: The sumptuous 'peony-flowered' form of
Papaver somniferum, *the opium poppy, is packed with
frilled petals in glowing shades of red or pink.*

*Title page: Using unusual containers for potting up plants,
here pelargoniums and pansies, is classic cottage style.*

*Copyright page: An exuberant arrangement of cottage
garden flowers, including foxgloves, campanulas,*
Lychnis coronaria *and Welsh poppies.*

CONTENTS

INTRODUCTION

Throughout the twentieth century, and increasingly in the latter half, interest in all forms of gardening has mushroomed as growing numbers of plant nurseries and garden centers have made an almost limitless range of plants readily available. Fashion trends in planting and landscaping may come and go, but the enduring appeal of the cottage garden remains. Perhaps because the pace of modern living is continually accelerating, the nostalgic dream of a leafy haven of dappled sunlight and tumbling swathes of flowers filled with sound and scent casts a more seductive spell than ever before... an oasis of enchantment and tranquillity removed from the techno-age rushing past the gate... a cottage garden...

Fortunately for the modern gardener, the term relates to the particular style of layout and plants and the mood created, rather than the accompanying building; few cottage gardens these days have the benefit of the picturesque dwelling, old walls and ancient trees of popular imagination. All gardening is a combination of artifice and management; in a good garden each element is as carefully designed and orchestrated as a piece of theatre to produce a desired effect (even that of untrammeled nature appearing untouched by human hand!). Therefore, with the aid and sensitive use of various devices it is possible to reproduce the atmosphere of the cottage garden even under the most adverse conditions.

This book provides ideas for enhancing any natural advantages, the means of disguising unavoidable eyesores - and even the possibility of transforming one into the other!

Left: A cottage garden planting of alliums, Jacob's ladder and cranesbill.   *Right:* Asiatic lilies, 'Pixie' hybrids.

The cottage garden concept

It would be impossible to imagine anything further removed from the riotous flower-filled delight of the cottage garden than the medieval peasant's squalid enclosure from which it grew. Cluttered with ramshackle sheds, pigsty, fowl pen, earth closet, washing and the general detritus of an overcrowded hovel, for centuries the only plants grown were feedstuff for family and animals and medicinal herbs. Eventually, as living conditions improved, the 'garden' was tidied up, fruit trees and beehives introduced and flowers with pest-repelling properties planted around the orderly rows of vegetables, while a wide range of herbs grown for culinary and domestic use mingled with wildflowers seeding in from the surrounding countryside.

Historically made to suit the slenderest purse, the cottage garden is a place of liberating informality where normal rules do not apply; trees can lean, flowers sprawl, steps twist, paths wind...its components are, as often as not, recycled materials and artefacts. It is the greenest of gardens and never grand or pretentious. (This also applies to the plants!) Having evolved over so many centuries, it seems unreasonable not to allow the cottage garden to adapt to the needs of the late twentieth century, when far fewer people grow their own vegetables and most gardens have a lawn - not something associated with the 'true' cottage garden. The old-style haphazard planting, where flowers seeded and wandered at will over most of the available space, is impractical by today's standards. The romantic tangle portrayed by Victorian painters would be past its best in a few weeks. There are the disadvantages of modern buildings to contend with as well: impenetrable concrete footings, drain and drainage pipes, inspection covers and the like, all taking up precious space and ugly to boot, plus, all too often, an unsympathetic outlook.

Wildflowers

Wildflower mixtures such as this one, featuring daisies, poppies and cornflowers, are not practical for the cottage garden, lacking substance and stamina. However, on pages 84-85 (Easy annuals) you can see how to achieve a light-hearted scatter of small flowers without the drawbacks of wild ones.

Below: Growing strawberries and other fruit in pots makes sense when small amounts are more practical. Near enough to the door to deter birds and high enough to defeat slugs, you can be sure of a healthy crop. Pages 52-53 offer further suggestions for suitable subjects.

Right: Lilac (Syringa) - *evocative in flower and the scent of springtime in cottage gardens. Look at flowering shrubs for all seasons on pages 54-55 and find fragrances on pages 74-75.*

Below: A clipped 'bay tree' is a *traditional charming feature of the cottage garden. Pages 58-59 show you how to achieve this result and pages 50-51 look at the herb garden, with easy-to-manage methods.*

This most popular lilac, Syringa 'Souvenir de Louis Späth', has been grown in country gardens for over a century.

Below: If you would like to copy this *delightful flight of easily and cheaply constructed steps, now so prettily colonized by creeping Jenny and other plants, turn to pages 26-27.*

Right: Sadly, bees are rarely kept in *cottage gardens these days, but if you have a disused beehive, pages 16-17 may stir your imagination to reincarnate it or other bygones.*

Hard landscaping

Think of your garden like a body. The 'bones' of the garden are the elements of hard landscaping. Get those right first and the rest will follow naturally. Before committing yourself to a definite plan, go out and stand in your plot and note its characteristics: the lie of the land, the nature of the local stone or rock (flint, sandstone, etc.) and any features you need to allow for when planning paths, walls or paving. If the ground is completely flat, it would probably benefit from the introduction of higher levels in the form of raised beds behind low retaining walls and a good paved area. If it is uneven, consider emphasizing the difference by means of terracing. Steeply sloping ground could provide a striking 'natural' rockery beside a flight of steps. Whatever the final plan, the hard landscaping will add immeasurably to the quality of the garden, but beware new bricks and concrete paving slabs.

The informality of cottage garden planting demands an equally informal approach to landscaping materials. You can use or reuse almost anything: old brick, cobbles, flint, stone, shingle, slate, tile and wood. Salvage usable stones when digging or shifting soil for reuse later on. Raised beds can be cheaply and attractively retained with wood used either as vertical posts or split and laid horizontally. Even if it is first treated with a suitable preservative, wood will rot after a few years, but it is easily replaced. Carry out the work a little at a time as the need arises to avoid too much disturbance.

Left: Here, old wooden railway sleepers have been used to make a small flight of steps. This wood is completely impregnated with preservative and lasts indefinitely.

Right: This is a clean and simple solution for a small area: a circle of red pavers laid in a circular gravel bed edged with old bricks brings out the beauty of the plants.

Even chunks of broken concrete can be useful, but only in moderation and never alone. In a damp shady place they quickly become green and mossy.

Old pantiles are useful as wall capping or path edging or incorporated into a random wall.

Flint cobbles. Dig them out of the garden if you are in the right area. If not, you are probably compensated with sandstone or granite.

Sea-worn shingle is more irregular in size than the quarried product and a better color, but much more expensive.

Natural slate is very heavy and therefore expensive if you have to buy it, but it is the perfect companion for shingle, flint or cobbles.

Right: The breath-taking blue of the tiles in this unusual path is echoed in the edging on top of the low fence. Note the way the brick path has been imaginatively laid, in flowing lines and curves rather than in a rigid pattern.

Modern concrete block paver. These are cheap and frostproof and the brown and brindled colors are much better than red and gray.

Old floor bricks are a lovely color, but will fly apart in the first frost if worn or damaged.

Modern iron-spot frostproof pavers are thinner than a brick. Good if used informally and mixed with other materials.

These reproduction facing bricks are very attractive but expensive. Nearest to the old handmade bricks in color.

These beach cobbles have beautiful soft colors and shapes. They look equally good with any other material, but are expensive if you cannot collect your own.

Below: *An attractive edging for a slab-and-shingled area made in the traditional manner from small pieces of sandstone set on edge.*

Right: *Broken pieces of riven slate are used creatively here, skilfully piled up to make a dry stone wall and steps. These set the magnificent display of foxgloves off to perfection and provide chinks and crevices for innumerable self-set seedlings.*

Creative recycling

Above: *The leafy plinth beneath this figure is in reality a disused garden roller detached from its handle and upended. Now it is smothered in ivy 'Buttercup' and Sedum 'Acre'.*

Economic necessity compelled early cottage gardeners to solve their problems in imaginative ways, using any means to hand. For instance, old boundary hedges were commonly reinforced with a startling variety of objects, from bedsteads and bicycles to tin trays and window frames. Obviously today's gardeners would not emulate tactics driven by poverty and lack of a waste disposal service, but the tradition can be maintained to introduce character and a note of humor to the garden, while making enormous savings and avoiding mass produced wares. Good, reclaimed building materials, however small the quantity, are always invaluable. Or utilitarian articles, such as an old-fashioned hand pump gushing into a half barrel that has been coated in pitch and sunk into the earth to complete the water feature. Left intact, a barrel is easily converted into a water butt or, given a cushion, an instant seat. Old animal feeders or drinking troughs provide endless possibilities for interesting reuse. Household bygones are tremendously adaptable. An old stool topped by a circular paving slab makes a useful small table by a garden chair. Intricate cast-iron bedends can be gracefully incorporated into seating or walling, while the ancient laundry copper, its rounded base nesting in a necklace of flint or cobbles, becomes a charming and capacious planter. Baskets lined with plastic make attractive if fairly shortlived potholders. Raise the base off the ground if you are not hanging them. Apart from the pleasure and satisfaction derived from making use of any interesting odds and ends, venerable artefacts perfectly capture the mood - but they must be used with caution, casually and unfussily, not displayed like museum pieces.

Edging with tiles

Small quantities of old roof tiles can be bought easily and cheaply and with little effort reused as an economical capping for walls or an edging for paths and beds in the cottage garden. Pantiles are particularly effective because of their interlocking curves. Using a masonry cutting disc on an electric drill you can cut them quickly and effortlessly without the risk of damage.

1 *Cut each pantile in half and bed the pieces into the soil, so that they overlap and the curves fit into each other, leaning slightly outwards.*

2 *Leave 3in(7.5cm) of the tile edges standing above soil level. Support them evenly on both sides and tread down gently to secure them.*

3 *When the entire surface of the path is firmed down, spread a layer of shingle, rake it lightly and tread it up against the tile faces.*

A plinth for an urn

An urn-shaped planting pot usually benefits from being raised on a plinth, which you can make yourself for almost nothing. If you visit your local garage, you should be able to obtain an empty plastic oil drum - one 19in(48cm) tall is more than large enough for the purpose.

1 Drain the drum and wash the outside with detergent, keeping it upside-down. Apply blackboard paint. Repeat an hour later.

2 When dry, stand in position and shorten if needed, either by cutting off the surplus or digging it into the soil. Place the urn on top.

A display of penstemons, nicotianas, petunias, verbenas and roses.

3 Plant an ivy close to the drum and fasten the tips down with modeling paste or small strips of strong tape. Pinch out the tips regularly to encourage spreading growth and clip when well grown.

'Lutzii' is a small-compact ivy with mottled variegation that acts as a foil for the flowers.

Left: The slanting edges of two broken sheets of slate are exploited to good effect by placing them above and below the square central piece, giving the illusion of curving steps to guide the walker round a corner.

Right: A huge old kettle linked to a small electric pump is transformed into a unique and amusing feature, pouring endlessly into the pool. An old cooking pot or jug would be equally intriguing.

Unusual containers

Any number of unusual and amusing bygones have been pressed into service as plant containers in the cottage garden, from boots and buckets to chimney pots and saucepans. Saucepans and buckets are a good shape, as they have relatively straight sides; if you intend to plant directly into them, remember to drill drainage holes in the base, but it is easier simply to stand a plant pot raised on a layer of shingle inside. However enticing, any shape that curves in too acutely at the top, such as a kettle, makes a poor container. Not only is the hole too small to accept a decent-sized flowerpot, but it is also difficult to give the plant sufficient water once its roots have spread inside.

The popularity of old kitchen sinks as containers for miniature alpine or Japanese gardens remains undiminished and even though the original stone sinks are no longer available, you can make an acceptable substitute by giving a more recent white-glazed sink a covering of hypertufa. Bind together equal parts of sand, cement and peat with water. Apply a coat of adhesive over the sink and after it has dried, press the mixture on with your hands. Leave the container to dry thoroughly before planting it up.

Traditional galvanized buckets are still produced and make good planters. You can give them an attractive matt black appearance by applying a coat of blackboard paint, which has the advantage of drying very quickly.

1 Apply the black paint evenly, retouching it where necessary after it has dried. Blackboard paint will dry in less than an hour.

2 Drill a hanging hole in the back. Support the bucket on end, with the straining cone downwards, and half fill it with garden soil.

3 Leave the plants in pots until they have grown on to ensure that they have enough light and water. Replant into the bucket, with potting mix, later.

Pelargonium 'Salmon Queen' (ivy-leaved trailing geranium)

Above: *Old leather boots acquire a new lease of life as home to a pretty mix of Ajuga 'Burgundy Glow' and Viola 'Purple Duet'.*

Below: *California poppies, Eschscholzia californica, make a stunning feature blooming in an old iron cooking pot on the patio.*

4 *Arrange the pots around the 'upper' half of the bucket, supporting the top pot if necessary to keep it well forward. Water well.*

5 *Hang the bucket on a screw or nail - remembering to hang the handle downwards - and keep it well-watered. Deadhead flowers regularly.*

Pansies in a metal bucket

1 *Here, the bucket is left unpainted and used as a pot holder. Put a layer of shingle on the base of the bucket to raise the base of the pot and improve drainage.*

2 *Choose a flowerpot with a diameter that fits comfortably inside the bucket. Plant it up with a selection of suitable plants and stand it on the bed of shingle.*

3 *The cheerful little viola 'Jackanapes', bred by Gertrude Jekyll, mixes well with a pansy of the same color combination.*

Informal paving

You can use almost any durable material for informal paving as long as it has an agreeable texture and appearance, is laid with care and is an integral part of a whole area. Apply the same design guidelines as you would to the layout of the garden or to the planting. Consider the entire area you wish to cover; if you have a large quantity of one or two materials - say, old bricks and pieces of flat rock - group them so that they appear at intervals throughout the whole space and fill in with patches of scarcer pieces. Always lay the largest pieces first and work down to the smallest, which helps to 'stitch' the rest together. The ground need not be completely flat, but it should be even. Bed the materials in well, so that there is no danger of anyone tripping or kicking out loose pieces. There may be a particular feature, such as a millstone, that you wish to emphasize or some attractive broken tiles or crockery. Consider anything and everything before making a start. If the area is large or very long, you may need to eke out the interesting pieces with a background of shingle or even carry out the work a bit at a time as circumstances allow.

The matt greens and blues of slate combine well with both garden flints and beach cobbles.

4 Space out groups of the larger materials evenly over the area to be covered. Bed them in firmly and make sure there are no raised edges.

1 First rake the ground to remove any debris and loosen and smooth the soil. Next, tread it down firmly and evenly with your heels, taking care not to leave 'pits' in the surface.

2 Lightly rake over a thin layer of clay pot pieces or pebbles and tread them down well, removing any surplus. All the hardcore must be bedded in, not overlapping and loose.

3 Choose the largest regular shapes to begin with. In this instance, all the materials are in small, fairly equal amounts, so each needs to form a group rather than be mixed up.

5 *If necessary, set pieces of broken concrete deeper into the ground to accommodate their uneven thickness. Put the rough face uppermost.*

6 *Fill in some of the gaps with the cobbles, keeping them at the same depth as the bricks and slabs that you have laid across the area.*

7 *Use shingle to fill the last of the gaps, building it up to match the level of the surrounding materials. Plants grow very well in shingle.*

Below: *Non-flowering chamomile 'Treneague' has grown thickly around and between these riven slabs. It is shorter than the flowering forms, equally aromatic and needs no mowing.*

Old clay floor tiles are worth seeking out, but expensive.

8 *If the area is not being planted, finish off by brushing sand between the flints and cobbles. It is easy to keep the surface clean with an occasional application of weedkiller.*

Plants for paths and paving

One of the prettiest features of the cottage garden is a carpet of low-growing plants in paths or paving. These divide roughly into three groups. Firstly, there are the larger mound-forming plants and dwarf shrubs, such as rock roses *(Helianthemum)*, lavender, catmint *(Nepeta)* and lady's mantle *(Alchemilla mollis)*, that lend a little height and substance to the edges. Next, are plants for paving, including saxifrage, phlox and dianthus, which form neat clumps and sprays that are not intended to be walked on. Lastly, there are the prostrate carpeters that tolerate considerable wear, such as the mat-forming thyme, *Thymus serpyllum*, and non-flowering *Chamomile* 'Treneague'. The indestructible *Leptinella potentillina* *(Cotula squalida)* is entirely maintenance-free, but use it on its own in a well-edged area; never forget that even among the daintiest of plants are those that become power-mad invaders once released in the garden - find out before you buy! Some of the most pernicious examples include certain *Oxalis, Sedum, Polygonum* and the deceptively fragile *Pratia pedunculata* and *Campanula poscharskyana*. Take care not to make your path or paved area into an obstacle course. Keep to the tiny crevice-dwellers and mat-forming subjects and plan a route that can be followed easily and naturally among them.

This tall, pretty saxifrage 'Triumph' has flowers of mixed red and pink.

Aubretia is trouble-free and flowers for weeks on end. 'Bob Saunders' is one of the deepest purples available.

Geranium cinereum 'Laurence Flatman' is reliable, compact and long flowering.

Dianthus 'Whatfield Joy' is one of many sturdy, fragrant little pinks among the alpines.

'Bressingham Pink' is one of the best-flowered prostrate thymes and brings in bees on a warm day.

Lithodora 'Heavenly Blue' needs acid soil around its roots. It is worth the trouble for its wonderful color.

Phlox douglasii will cover quite a stretch - good on a bank or over a low wall.

Neat, easy Sedum spathulifolium 'Purpureum' has deep, glowing, pink-red flowers.

Few plants are smaller than Saxifraga cochlearifolia minor 'Pixie'. Give it a little shelter.

Alpines, such as this Dianthus 'Garland', growing in a clay pan, make good accent plants.

Left: *Plain or variegated thymes are equally good in cookery. All do well in a sunny place in shingle or paving to keep them well drained in winter. This is 'Bressingham Pink'.*

1 This lovely Oxalis adenophylla furls its flowers like a closed umbrella when not in full sun. Plant it where it will not be damaged.

2 When planting tiny or delicate plants, finish off with a few handfuls of grit. It protects them from slugs and keeps them well drained.

Above: *These small geraniums are good at the edges of paving. They need more gentle conditions and plenty of moisture-retaining potting mixture in the planting pocket.*

23

Garden pathways

In the planning stage, when you are determining the position of the various areas in your garden, give careful thought to the route that will link them all. You may decide on a formally straight path in the old-fashioned style, edged, for example, with lavender or catmint, or one that curves away invitingly, beckoning you to sights unseen. Whatever your choice, the path is a major element in the garden - the spine in the framework of the body - and of considerable value in establishing mood.

Below: Strongly scented chamomile (Anthemis) surrounds the stones in this path, the center being mown occasionally to keep it compact. The non-flowering form, Chamaemelum nobile *'Treneague', is prostrate and needs no cutting.*

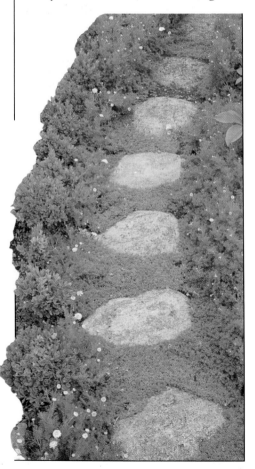

There is a huge range of surfacing materials to choose from according to your pocket and inclination, beginning with beaten earth compacted with grit and pebbles that costs virtually nothing, through grass, shingle or bark, to brick and all forms of natural stone plus any combination of the above. Whatever the treatment, the path needs to be comfortable to use in terms of its surface, its width and the space allowed above it. There should be space for two people to walk side by side or for you to maneuver a wheelbarrow, etc. Although the thought of brushing through sweetly scented leaves and flowers on a hot afternoon might seem appealing, you will quickly get unpleasantly wet if it has been raining.

A path must always lead somewhere, even when it is not purely functional - to a seat, a view or a pot. Made wide enough, it will provide the perfect site for groups of plants in pots, for showing off a cherished specimen or planting underfoot. Shingle around the house is especially good, as all the favorite garden plants love it and you can develop a profusion of plants and climbers against the walls without having beds. A stepping stone path through a wide border allows access for maintenance without having to tread on and compact the soil.

Above: The perfect path, open and inviting, winds between skilfully planted borders of mixed plants and shrubs. A beautifully stitched together garden to look good in all seasons.

Right: This attractive and informal path is made of slate shale contained by irregular pieces of flat rock laid on edge. Where available, this material makes the easiest possible surface.

A gravel walkway with brick patterns

1 Rake the ground to remove any debris, level it and tread it down. Cover the compacted earth with a good layer of moistened sand and flatten it down. Lay a line of bricks from side to side, level with the side edges. Pavers set on edge are neater for the sides, but be sure to make them firm and level.

2 Fill the triangular spaces with shingle and tread it down gently so as not to push the edging out of line before it has settled.

3 Edge this simple but effective formal path with suitable plants. The path is cheap and easy to make and there is no need to cut the bricks.

The urn provides a focal point at the end of the path.

Below: This cobble and brick path could be laid in stages - and the impressive terracotta pot could travel with it as each section is completed.

1 To make a flight of rustic steps, choose reasonably substantial, well-matched branches or larch poles if 'natural' wood is not available.

Steps along the way

Wherever different levels are planned, it is likely that steps will be needed, either as a continuous flight or spread apart singly over a distance, depending on the rise of the ground. Steps can make a charming feature and children love them, but for both appearance and safety's sake, they need to be shallow, wide and deep. One of the commonest mistakes is to make them with similar dimensions to a staircase, which for outdoors is far too steep and narrow; it is impossible to stroll in comfort up steps with risers that are more than 5in(13cm) high, and there should be ample space on the tread from front to back. Bear in mind that the leading edge can be curved inwards as well as outwards, or the whole step can be completely asymmetric at its most informal and made of an even more diverse range of materials than the path - but here again, steer clear of the brutality of concrete. The garden can benefit greatly from attractive steps used both to link and separate areas, while providing a feature in themselves. Even where the ground is almost flat, you can create direction and an illusion of depth by cutting a long step into a lawn. Two or three winding steps will transform a sharp corner, one or two add importance to an archway, one makes a raised base for a special seat.

2 Dig a shelf or groove the full length of the first piece of timber, deep enough to prevent it slipping when you put your weight on it.

3 Fill in any space beneath the piece of timber with the loose soil and pack it in tightly to prevent the ground being eroded by rain.

4 Knock in a peg of preserved softwood about 10-12in(25-30cm) long, a few inches in from each end to just above half the depth of the log.

5 Judge the distance to the next step and dig out the slope, pulling the soil back behind the timber. If the steps are to wind, cut out a wedge shape.

6 Compact the loose soil by treading it hard down with your heels. It is most important to make each step completely stable as you lay it.

7 Having dug a groove and laid the next piece of timber firmly in place, rake the area to level the surface just below the top of the first step.

8 When you have finished laying the required number of steps and pegged them in position, complete the project with a generous layer of fairly coarsely chipped bark. Rake it over and tread down.

You may need to scoop some earth from behind each step to lodge the bark.

There will be some sinkage at first. Rake aside the bark to top up the area with soil and then replenish the bark.

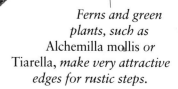

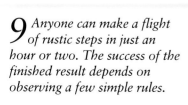

9 Anyone can make a flight of rustic steps in just an hour or two. The success of the finished result depends on observing a few simple rules.

Ferns and green plants, such as Alchemilla mollis or Tiarella, make very attractive edges for rustic steps.

Pots of plants

Pot plants are the gardener's ever-present help in time of need, whether it is to conceal and transform an eyesore into a stunning focal point, plump up a tired flower bed, or bring impact to a dull area. They also provide an opportunity for growing specimens unsuited to your conditions; because their requirements are individually catered for, you can grow virtually anything you wish. In general, pots in a group should be of the same color and material - terracotta for example - and fairly plain. You can, of course, paint an assortment of pots to achieve a matching appearance. Small pots and bowls work effectively for dot plants, but where pots are grouped together use fewer and larger containers, otherwise the result is an untidy and unsatisfactory muddle. Remember that the smaller the pot the faster it dries out. At the top end of the market are the exquisite handmade Greek pithoi, too beautiful in themselves to need plants in them. Reproduction period urns and tubs, better used alone or as a pair, lend themselves to foliage plants, such as hostas, or the felted silver or soft lime leaves of *Helichrysum petiolatum*, perhaps planted with single blue petunias or white trailing pelargoniums. Dot plants are fun; try experimenting with some of the smaller perennials, such as *Heuchera*, or the slow, clump-forming grasses and ferns. Give larger pots some protection from frost by raising them on small clay feet. However, if not guaranteed frostproof, there is no certainty that they will not shatter unless made of plastic.

Plants for pots 12in (30cm) and more

Pieris, *azalea and dwarf* Rhododendron. *Plant these in ericaceous potting mixture and keep in partial shade.*

Ferns, grasses and hostas. Keep them moist and in light shade.

Agapanthus, *species gladioli,* Nerine *and species tulips. These bulbs require sharp drainage and a sunny site.*

Argyranthemum 'Jamaica Primrose', *bay trees,* Bidens aurea, Chaenomeles 'Simonii', Felicia amelloides *and* Osteospermum *need sun.*

1 *Select a good-sized pot and place a few pieces of broken clay pot or pebbles in the base to prevent the drainage hole getting blocked.*

2 *Half-fill the pot with good-quality potting mixture. If you have chosen really acid-loving lilies, be sure to plant them in an ericaceous mix.*

3 *Slide your fingers between the stems to support the plant without damage. Upend the pot and tap the base to shake the root free safely.*

Asiatic hybrids are short, easy and lime-tolerant. Buy bulbs directly from growers.

'Denia Pixie'

4 *Supporting the roots with both hands, place the plant gently on the potting mixture. Follow the same procedure for the other lilies, spacing them equally.*

'Buff Pixie'

'Orange Pixie'

5 *Carefully fill up the spaces between the stems with potting mixture. Firm it gently with your fingers and water the container. If any depressions appear, fill them with more potting mixture.*

6 *Lilies need to be looked after if they are to flourish; water and feed them on a regular basis. Do not overwater them, but do not let them become dried out, especially by wind.*

29

Chimney pots as planters

Chimney pots, both old and new, make a striking display when used in groups of varying styles and height. When planting a tall container of this sort, it is better to find a plastic plant pot (or bucket) large enough to lodge in the top. If you fill the chimney itself with soil, it will become too dry and compacted to support a healthy plant - and also immovable. Look at your chimney pot both ways up before deciding how to use it; many, especially the tall ones, are a better shape upside-down and more effective planted this way, because being wider at the base, they will hold a larger pot. The height of the chimney will dictate the type of plants to grow in it; the tallest ones look better with plants that flow out and down, such as ivy or trailing geraniums. There are also plenty of tender perennials to choose from. Short, stubby little pots look equally good with erect, bushy or trailing plants, such as *Phormium*, grasses, *Hosta* and *Helianthemum*.

It is often a great help to be able to raise a group of plants in, or at the back of, the flower bed for those times when there is a gap in the flowering succession, or to keep it going when it is past its best. With their narrow, straight lines, the tall chimney pots are excellent used in this way.

1 In this instance, the chimney pot has been reversed. Choose a flowerpot with a suitable diameter to lodge inside the rim.

A hosta in a short chimney pot

1 Because this is only a short pot - just 12in (30cm) high - it does not need to be lined with a flowerpot before you start planting it up.

2 Two-thirds fill with a mixture of good-quality soil and potting mixture or potting mixture alone.

2 Put a few broken crocks in the bottom of the flowerpot to improve drainage, and add potting mixture until it is two-thirds full.

3 Place the first plant well over to one side of the pot, so that it leans outwards a little. Cover the roots with a small amount of potting mixture.

3 Gently tease out and separate the roots and then place the plant in the pot. Water it in, fill up with potting mix and water again.

4 Position the remaining plants around the pot in the same way. Generously fill the spaces between them with potting mixture, firm down and water well.

The gracefully drooping stems of Osteospermum 'Sunny Girl', 'Sunny Boy' and 'Langtrees' are perfect for a tall pot or urn.

The scarlet Pelargonium 'Mars' in a modern 'cannon-head' 18in(45cm) pot.

Golden Helichrysum petiolatum will spread out and down to balance Pelargonium 'Knaufs Bonfire' and salmon-pink Geranium 'Rokoko'.

Hosta fortunei aureomarginata *has fragrant spikes of lavender flowers in summer. Keep it moist and cool.*

Above: *With their clean lines and architectural presence, chimney pots make ideal plant holders used together or individually for height and emphasis.*

Creeping Jenny Lysimachia nummularia 'Aurea' in a small pot. Keep it out of strong sun and wind or it will scorch.

Grass in the garden

Historically, a grassed area was not a part of the cottage garden; making precious space unproductive would simply not have been thought of before the mower was invented. Today, lawns provide a soft and restful setting for the plants and the cheapest and easiest means of acquiring a durable surface. Although grass needs a great deal of maintenance, its demands are offset by its adaptability and the modern strimmer, which can cut in hitherto impractical places. Do not try to grow grass in heavy shade or where drainage is poor or it will be sparse and weak and invaded by moss. Keep the shape soft for the most part, with irregular edges fading away into low shrubs or drifts of flowers. A smooth, undulating surface makes an attractive lawn for a cottage garden and helps to give an illusion of space to a confined area where straight edges and a flat surface would accentuate it. Grass is excellent used as a fluid, free-flowing shape - not as narrow or precise as a path - that reaches and links all parts of the garden. Bald patches may be caused by wear on grass paths or by the foliage of plants closely overhanging the lawn through the summer months. A lasting remedy for the problem with paths is to cut the odd stepping stone into the turf at vulnerable points. For bare edges under plants, you will need several small slabs side-by-side. If their color is too bright, matt finish floor paint mixed in a neutral or slate-colored shade will make them almost unnoticeable.

For lower maintenance, leave an area of grass to produce wildflowers and mow it only a few times a year.

Above: Small concrete paving slabs have been set in to protect the edge of this turf, already suffering from drought. Slate-colored floor paint makes them less conspicuous.

Right: The grass disappears under the clumps of flowers at the front of this beautiful border. The mower will nudge into them without damage - and there is no edging to do!

Below: The quality of the grass may suffer under these ornamental trees. It helps to naturalize spring bulbs and wildflowers in these areas and leave them unmown until late summer.

Above: Natural 'stepping stones' in this lawn prevent worn patches by the steps and provide a dry path when the turf is wet. They must not stand higher than the soil surface.

Below: The early flowering season of crocuses means that they have usually died down before the lawn needs its first spring mowing, and they can increase undisturbed.

Improving the boundaries

The boundaries of the old cottage gardens served mainly as animal restraints. Today they are required to provide shade and shelter as well as an aesthetically pleasing backdrop. If your plot is surrounded by fencing you can disguise it by concealing and breaking up the distracting horizontal lines. This is best done in a variety of ways, not merely planting an unbroken series of climbers along it. Try extending the height in places with a rustic or strong trellis panel to accommodate a substantial climber, such as Rose 'Albertine', or grow a length of hedge against part of the fence, allowing one of the hedging plants to grow up from the clipped ones at various intervals. Should you have no room for a hedge, make a fedge; growing ivy to cover the fence completely, and then keeping it clipped. In this instance stick to one, preferably green, variety. Plant a loose and informal mix of shrubs and small trees varying in height and color, in irregular groups along a stretch of fence, deceiving the eye into forgetting the boundary exists. If you prefer a traditional hedge, there are several species to choose from; for the cottage garden, avoid fast-growing conifers at all costs. Hawthorn, yew, beech and briar are suitable subjects, becoming high and wide with clipping. A mixed planting is most attractive and less formal, especially if clipped in undulating curves outlining the individual shapes within it, but refrain from using strongly contrasting colored foliage.

Above: A simple opening in this tall hedge of traditional beech makes an unusual and charming front entrance to this country garden.

Right: Viburnum tinus *makes an excellent screen; evergreen for privacy and wind shelter, easy and healthy and flowering all winter. It also responds well to clipping.*

Above: Euonymus 'Emerald Gaiety' *will climb without assistance if grown against a tree or fence. Here, it is weaving with a honeysuckle through a trellis panel to conceal a row of sheds.*

Apply this technique to dwarf, red-leaved Prunus cistena. For ash (Fraxinus) leave upstanding trees unclipped.

Plants for internal boundaries

Internal boundaries need to be on a smaller scale than the external ones. Potentilla, lavender (shown right), senecio, tall catmint and cotton lavender are some of the flowering shrubs that make delightful dwarf hedges and need only light trimming to keep them compact.

Below: *The dwarf habit and long flowering season of the 'County' roses makes them ideal for a small hedge. Prune very lightly.*

'Surrey'

'Avon'

'Suffolk'

Above: *This pleasing cottage garden hedge illustrates a method that was popular last century. Here, different colored hawthorns (Crataegus) have been used to good effect.*

Left: *Clematis 'Victoria' drapes a blanket of flower over this simple cottage fence. Because it is cut back hard every winter, it will not out-grow its low support.*

Ivy in its place

Gardeners could make far more use of the ivies, given the diversity of the range; they are available in shades of green, cream, gold and gray. The rampant large-leaved varieties, such as 'Gloire de Marengo', 'Sulphur Heart' (syn. 'Paddy's Pride') and *H. colchica dentata* 'Variegata', should be used with caution, as they need ample space. Of the many forms of *Hedera helix*, common ivy, two of the best for the cottage garden are the softly variegated gray-green-and-white 'Glacier', neat and reliable in full sun, and 'Buttercup', clear shining yellow in spring, fading to green-gold later in the year. 'Green Ripple' is a good, plain, green cultivar with interesting leaves, equally suitable for a wall or ground cover, as is the fast-growing, narrow, arrow-shaped 'Sagittifolia'. Many ivies do not climb; some are free-standing shrubs, such as the handsome 'Arborescens Variegata', that slowly reaches 6-8ft (2-2.5m), given protection from cold winds, and produces attractive clusters of flowers and berries. 'Erecta' is an intriguing small shrub at 39in(1m) high. Its stiffly upright branches lined with small, darkly glossy curved leaves, make an effective focal point. Mound-forming ivies are particularly good as ground cover in small gardens and excellent for containers, perhaps to conceal a drain cover where you do not wish to restrict access. The vigorous 'Manda's Crested' and 'Cristata' and slower-growing 'Ivalace' are all contenders, while 'Little Diamond' makes a tidy hummock of variegated green and ivory, with blunt diamond-shaped leaves.

H. h. 'Manda's Crested' is happy where not too dry. After a slow start, it makes a strong, spreading carpet of foliage.

H. h. 'Ivalace' builds up the intricate elegant growth its name implies. It does not cling but can be bound on a post and clipped. Quite slow in dry ground.

The running shoots of H. h. 'Sagittifolia' will race away as soon as the plant is settled. Pinch out the tips to encourage it to thicken up.

H. h. 'Green Ripple' is an unobtrusive background ivy, capable of clothing a sizeable area of ground or wall. Easy to control where necessary.

Left: *A coating of hypertufa (page 18) has given an ivy the footing it needed to get a grip on this modern brick seat. If you plant ivy in a windy site, attach the stems to their support at first, by any means available.*

H. h. 'Glacier' is a true classic. Bright young growth dulls to a soft gray-green, excellent where a change from green and yellow is needed.

H. h. 'Buttercup' is loved at first sight for its radiant unvariegated color. It shines out from half shade but will stand direct sun without scorching if not too dry.

H. h. 'Goldchild' is slow, slender, neat and easy. Its short flexible shoots are ideal for twining through a trellis.

H. h. 'Midas Touch' is a striking new ivy with strong green-and-gold marbling on polished leaves and unique copper-pink stems. Beware of overusing it.

The elegantly waved and beautifully colored leaves of H. h. 'Clotted Cream' are best displayed climbing through a tall shrub. Its slender habit will not inhibit its hosts' growth.

Keep H. h. 'Lutzii' small and neat, as the muddled variegation is not attractive in large amounts. An accommodating, compact, small-leaved ivy.

Above: *H. h. 'Erecta' has an attractive 'architectural' appearance, good for associating with rocks or statuary. It is an extremely slow-growing variety.*

Below: *H. h. 'Chrysophylla' bound and clipped on a section of post-and-rail fence, turns brilliant yellow in spring when covered in young growth.*

Left: *Although this is a clinging ivy, it has been wired onto the fence rail to prevent it becoming top heavy and blown off in the wind. It requires clipping only three times a year.*

Looking at archways

There can be no more useful element than the versatile archway to establish the mood of the cottage garden. Most popularly it spans a path, an open and inviting doorway to the mysteries glimpsed beyond, and as you pass through, delighting the senses with its blooms and scent. However, an arch can be used in other and varied ways and constructed from a range of materials. When planning the garden, look for any existing features that might be adapted to become an arch, say by tying the flexible limbs of two small trees together or cutting an opening in a tall clipped hedge. Or use an arch as a frame, rather than a doorway, to emphasize a seat or statue. However employed, the reason for it - visually - must be valid. Its mood can vary from the restful greens of an ivy-clad structure to an exuberant mix of flowering climbers. An archway can provide instant height, an easy means of dividing an area and an ideal support for the romantic cottage garden climbers - all at the same time! Be sure to allow sufficient space for the plants that the arch is to support. Almost all climbers are vigorous and bulky, so the frame needs to have sufficient depth as well as height and width and, especially with roses, enough overhead members to tie in new growth - it is no fun being swiped in the face by a thorny branch! If it is not to be swamped once the climbers are established, an archway should have a minimum internal measurement of 7ft high x 5ft wide x 3ft deep (2.1x1.5x1m). All this size is accompanied by considerable weight - be sure that all the elements of your arch are generously proportioned and stable.

Above: Hawthorn is a most successful subject for training into an arch. Flexible and tough, it can be bent and tied in to form attractive curves if extra height is needed.

Left: Euonymus 'Emerald Gaiety' and Hedera colchica dentata 'Variegata' form a pleasing evergreen archway over a gap in a wall. Ferns and hellebores grow at the base.

Building an archway entrance

The owners of this garden have all the problems common to modern building developments: deep, concrete foundations, intrusive drain covers and looming neighboring walls. However, they are determined to start making a cottage garden.

1 An archway is to be built into the gap between the corner of the house and the boundary fence to provide a gated entrance to the back garden and frame the view with flowers and foliage.

Left: *A simple wooden arch made of trellis panels supports the huge rose 'Albertine' at the end of a path prettily bordered by rose 'Ballerina', geraniums, marguerites, sisyrinchium and silver pyrethrum.*

Right: *Golden hop,* Humulus lupulus *'Aureus', reaches over the path to hang onto a convenient tree, forming a natural asymmetric archway in the summer. The hop dies to the ground in winter.*

2 *Stout wooden ledges 9in (23cm) wide are built in on each side of the gate to hold a row of pots containing trailing plants. Sturdy hinges are needed to hold up the gate.*

3 *Trellis panels are constructed in and on either side of the gate to restrain the dog while keeping the feeling of airiness and space. The structure is painted with preservative.*

4 *The first climber, Vitis 'Apiifolia', is planted. This young parsley-leaved vine is already bearing bunches of grapes that will be both decorative and edible in time.*

5 *The archway is high and wide enough to support several climbers apart from the vine. It will provide the leafy entrance to a secret garden that shuts out the modern world.*

Climbing plants

There is a wealth of climbing plants to cater for every need. Some, such as the mile-a-minute plant, or Russian vine, *Fallopia baldschuanicum*, or the glorious golden hop, *Humulus lupulus* 'Aureus', will throw a blanket of foliage over unsightly sheds or garages. *Wisteria sinensis*, on the other hand, adds elegance to a pergola or high wall. Climbing with a tall rose or the Etruscan honeysuckle, *Lonicera etrusca*, the fast and leggy *Solanum jasminoides* 'Album' will send a cascade of soft white flowers up two stories in a couple of seasons. Also for a sunny wall, the passion flower, *Passiflora caerulea*, is vigorous and untidy, but the exotically intricate flowers and associated mythology never fail to excite interest.

The exquisitely scented jasmine has been associated with the cottage garden for 500 years, but it does require a great deal of space in a sunny spot. There is also a striking variegated cultivar of the white-flowered *Jasminum officinale*. Magnificent on a shady wall, the woody, slow-to-establish *Hydrangea petiolaris* will eventually climb to the eaves with its scented lacecap creamy-white flowers in summer. Two vigorous hardy climbers that should be better known for their beautiful foliage are *Akebia quinata*, which has soft green leaves and small, scented, dusky purple flowers in spring, and *Celastrus orbiculatus*. Its crisp, clear green leaves turn a radiant yellow in the fall before dropping to leave clusters of small, golden seed capsules, each split to reveal the orange-red berry inside.

Right: The semi-evergreen Akebia quinata *will scramble through a tree without assistance, but as it does not cling it will need support on a wall. It is a very good subject for pergolas.*

Below: Fremontodendron californicum *is a vigorous woody shrub with good blue-green leathery leaves. It is capable of covering the largest wall, but has to be trained and tied in to keep it under control.*

Left: The vigorous climber Fallopia baldschuanicum *can ultimately cover an area of 60ft(18m), whether you like it or not. The Russian vine is a delight when in bloom in late summer.*

40

Right: 'Moroccan Broom', Cytisus battandieri, *is not actually a climber. However, it is more effective loosely trained against a sunny wall. It has silky, silvery leaves and pineapple-scented flowers in summer.*

Plant together with Clematis macropetala *'Markham's Pink' for a beautiful color combination.*

Left: Solanum jasminoides *'Album' is a lovely but leggy climber that needs to sprawl through a tall companion, such as* Magnolia grandiflora, *or be tied to a framework of wires.*

Tying in climbers

Campsis *hybrid 'Madame Galen' is the hardiest of a family of self-clinging climbers. They need support when young, so tie the stems to encourage spread and continue to tie in shoots.*

Garden climbers

Actinidia kolomikta, *variegated green/pink/white, sun, on wires.*
Eccremocarpus scaber, *yellow, orange or red tubular flowers, sun, scrambles on support.*
Euonymus *'Silver Queen', variegated green/cream leaves, any situation, self supporting.*
Parthenocissus henryana, *pink/silver veining on green, moderate size, good fall color, self supporting.*
Solanum crispum *'Glasnevin', yellow-centered purple flowers, sun, tie to wires or trellis.*
Wisteria *'Issai', blooms on young plants. Moderate size, sun, tie to wires.*

Ornamental trees

Typically, an ancient gnarled apple or plum tree would be seen to capture the mood of the cottage garden, providing shade and shelter for person and plant alike, and a crop of fruit in the process. Modern fruit trees however, grown on dwarf rootstocks, are too short to sit beneath and better replaced by the smaller ornamental trees, as long as they have a relaxed and natural habit. Among the huge *Prunus* family, covering almond, apricot, peach and cherry, are the very best flowering trees, many coloring well in the fall.

Similarly small trees of graceful habit, rivalling the *Prunus* for beauty, are the crab apples, *Malus*, profuse in blossom and fruits, which on some varieties last well into the winter. The cornelian cherry, *Cornus mas*, is a dense and twiggy small tree smothered with small yellow flowers on bare wood in winter and edible red cherrylike fruit in the fall. For a completely different effect, some of the cotoneasters make striking small trees with elegant arching branches, handsome corrugated leaves and large clusters of red berries. *C. bullatus,* with its rich fall color, and the semi-evergreen *C. frigidus* 'Cornubia', weighed down by its lavish crop of fruits, are notable examples. Two small weeping trees, very attractive if kept pruned to prevent them drooping to the ground and becoming too dense, are the silver pear, *Pyrus salicifolia* 'Pendula', and silver birch, *Betula pendula* 'Youngii'. Never be tempted to plant a weeping willow in a small garden as they become too large, with troublesome roots. When choosing the site for a tree consider the alteration in the micro-climate that its shade and roots will bring about.

Right: Its common name, golden rain, accurately describes the beautiful drooping habit of the laburnum. 'Vossii' is the most elegant form. All are extremely poisonous.

Above: Prunus mume 'Beni-chidore' is a superb Japanese apricot with very fragrant double, cupped flowers in rich pink to brighten late winter days.

Right: Prunus subhirtella 'Autumnalis', the winter-flowering cherry, produces flush after flush of pink-tinged flowers from the fall to late spring, and a light canopy of leaves in summer.

Left: *This lovely Japanese cherry Prunus 'Shogetsu' spreads a canopy of late spring blossom. The pink-tinged white flowers are large and double, strung gracefully along the wide-spreading branches on long stalks.*

Below: *Malus floribunda, the 'Japanese Crab' is one of the earliest and most beautiful. Spectacular masses of bloom form a textured tapestry of red and pink in spring as crimson buds open blush-pink and white. Small red and yellow crab apples follow in the fall.*

Left: *Sorbus cashmiriana is a lovely rowan for a small garden, with an open habit, pink flowers in late spring and gleaming white berries hanging on the branches after the colorful fall leaves have dropped. S. vilmorinii is equally choice, with gracefully spreading ferny foliage and rosy-pink-flushed white fruit.*

Shade under trees

Shady areas under trees provide perfect conditions for a host of plants that are unable to stand exposure to hot sun and drying winds. Be sure to dig in plenty of good moisture-retaining materials, such as leaf mold or coir compost, when planting. If the shade is very dense and dry - as under an evergreen - ivy might provide the only answer; kept trimmed, to thicken and contain its edges, it makes a most attractive carpet. A slow but delightful carpeter that will cope with shade is *Asarum europaeum*, which, with small, round, shining evergreen leaves at only 6in(15cm) high, could be underplanted with spring bulbs.

Ferns that do not need a great deal of moisture look cool and beautiful in light shade with wild columbines and cranesbill, *Geranium phaeum* (the mourning widow), in both its purple and white forms. Suitable ferns include *Athyrium pictum* and A. 'Minutissimum', *Blechnum penna-marina* and *Polypodium* 'Cornubiense'. Shady conditions are also ideal for early-flowering polyanthus and primrose-type primulas.

A group of beautiful foliage plants, reliable under deciduous trees and shrubs, includes *Tolmeia, Pachyphragma, Heuchera cylindrica, Tellima* and *Tiarella*. All are evergreen, some becoming red or purple-tinted in winter, and the last three have spikes of tiny flowers in cream or creamy pink. For brighter-colored flowers, try violas, ajugas, the fragrant stoloniferous phlox, dicentras, foxgloves, hostas, brunnera and bergenia. The compact spurge *Euphorbia robbiae* has dark leaves and yellow spring flowers.

The floriferous hellebore hybrid 'Heartsease'. Ideal for planting under trees in light soil with plenty of humus around the roots.

Above: Bergenia 'Baby Doll' is a smaller-scale plant than other 'elephant ears'. Its flower spikes at only 12in(30cm) high and neater leaves make it better ground cover.

Left: Tiarella cordifolia, *aptly named the foam flower, with glossy-leaved* Pachysandra. *Together they make an unbroken green carpet beneath a large tree.*

All the pinky reds and purples of this collection of Primula 'Wanda' hybrids blend beautifully together.

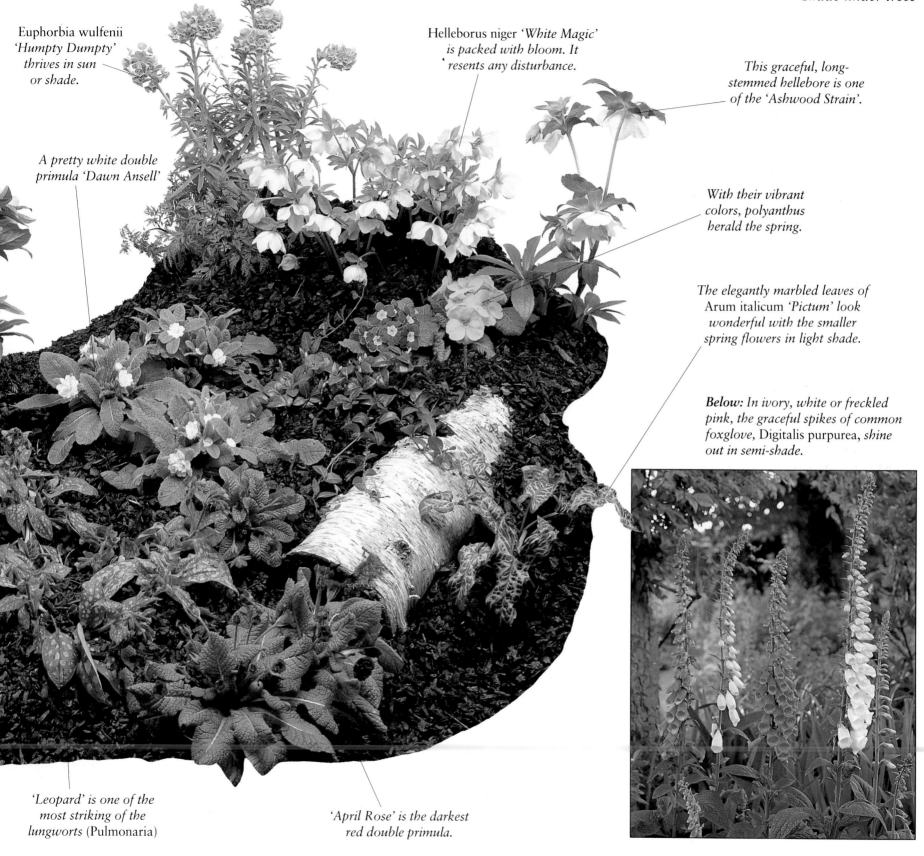

Euphorbia wulfenii
'*Humpty Dumpty*'
*thrives in sun
or shade.*

Helleborus niger '*White Magic*'
*is packed with bloom. It
resents any disturbance.*

*This graceful, long-
stemmed hellebore is one
of the 'Ashwood Strain'.*

*A pretty white double
primula 'Dawn Ansell'*

*With their vibrant
colors, polyanthus
herald the spring.*

*The elegantly marbled leaves of
Arum italicum '*Pictum*' look
wonderful with the smaller
spring flowers in light shade.*

Below: *In ivory, white or freckled
pink, the graceful spikes of common
foxglove,* Digitalis purpurea, *shine
out in semi-shade.*

'*Leopard*' *is one of the
most striking of the
lungworts (Pulmonaria)*

'*April Rose*' *is the darkest
red double primula.*

45

Spring bulbs

It seems remarkable that the first flowers to emerge at the end of the winter are among the smallest and most delicately formed of all - some even appearing from under the snow. Spring as a season is very variable, yet sooner or later, with total reliability, starting with the golden display of the winter aconite, *Eranthis hyemalis*, and continuing through to the tulips three months later, comes the glorious pageant of flowers provided by the spring bulbs. Their only drawback is that you may be tempted to fill the garden with them, quite overlooking the fact that to keep the bulbs in good heart you should not remove their copious foliage until it is wilting - six weeks after the flowers have faded. By this time it has become a serious obstacle in the flower bed. Furthermore, healthy bulbs are prolific breeders and increase rapidly, which can be a problem if there is not enough space to isolate them. As many bulbs are very small, they are too easily disturbed and damaged or lost if planted among herbaceous plants. Fortunately, there are places ideally suited to their needs where they can be left in peace without taking precious space from later flowerers. Most spring bulbs do well under deciduous trees and shrubs, where they bloom before the canopy of leaves unfolds to cut out the light. The majority, including daffodils, narcissi, bluebells, snowdrops, *Cyclamen coum* and the magnificent *Fritillaria imperialis*, enjoy the well-drained conditions of such a site and can be left undisturbed for years.

Left: To avoid the attentions of predatory animals, these pretty tulips 'Pink Frills' are pot grown.

Miniature Narcissus juncifolius. *A blend of narcissi and daffodils form luminous pools of color and perfume. By choosing varieties with care, you can extend the flowering period over several weeks.*

Crocus tomasinianus *is one of the earliest crocuses to bloom.*

Plant tiny Iris reticulata *in pockets of well-fed, light, gritty soil.*

The single snowdrop, Galanthus nivalis, *is more graceful than the double form.*

A cool, well-drained site suits the charming Anemone blanda.

Late winter-flowering Cyclamen coum *ranges from white to deep red. Some named varieties have marbled or silver leaves.*

Daffodil 'Baby Moon'

Discarded indoor hyacinths will go on for years in the garden, given a quiet corner where they can be left undisturbed and kept clear of encroaching plants.

Ranunculus ficaria *'Brazen Hussy', an appealing bronze-leaved celandine that romps about true to its name!*

Above: *One of the prettiest anemones, blanda's daisylike flowers light up in partial shade at the base of a tree.*

The common double snowdrop Galanthus nivalis *'Flore Pleno' increases rapidly.*

Below: Leucojum vernum, *the spring snowflake, is closely related to the snowdrop, but blooms in spring. In moist ground it will make a substantial 8in(20cm) clump. The summer snowflake, L. aestivum, is taller and blooms later.*

Plant the grape hyacinth, Muscari armeniacum, *in full sun. The double 'Blue Spike' has a very long flowering period.*

A seat with a view

It is worth making the most of your garden by carefully siting vantage points at which to sit and reflect upon the view. Deciding where to have the seating is one of the most enjoyable aspects of creating a garden; there are so many possibilities, from a paved area with tables and chairs to assorted perches on which to ruminate with a leisurely drink. Remember that the views back to the house are just as important as looking out from it, so site some seats accordingly. The secret of successful seating is to make it inviting and comfortable, and furnish the garden with points of interest protected from the prevailing wind (with an alternative option should it blow from a different quarter!) Provide a seat in the sun, as well as in the shade, and a surface for a cup and plate. If the fabric of the seat retains moisture, add some cushions. Cost is a matter of personal choice. A covering of hypertufa (equal parts of sand, cement and peat) will give a cheap brick and concrete built-in seat the instant appearance of old stone. You could incorporate a seat into a stretch of low walling or build one into a slope and plant it with chamomile or thyme for a sensationally scented feature - though beware of ants with the former and bees at flowering time with the latter.

1 Some garden centers stock inexpensive softwood seats. If they have not already been treated, paint them with a good-quality brand of wood preservative that will not fade and is water repellent.

Below: A peaceful retreat at the back of the garden. From this inviting rustic bench you can enjoy all the scents of the herbs and the myriads of winged visitors attracted to them.

Left: This small seat was formed by scooping a slice out of a slightly sloping lawn and mounding the soil up at the back until it was high enough to support the brick-work, where purple ivy-leaved toadflax and Welsh poppies have found a welcome home.

2 Unless the seat is to stand on paving, place a slab or brick under each leg. Put these in position and cut round the lawn with an old knife.

3 Take out enough turf and soil to allow for a bed of sand beneath each slab, so that you can level them with the surface and with each other.

4 Bring the two halves of the seat together, making sure that the legs are correctly placed on their bases. It is easy to make adjustments at this stage.

A taller version of this structure makes a charming garden table as seated people face inwards, rather than out.

5 Thread the bolts, each with a washer on, through their respective holes. Add another washer before the nut to prevent it biting into the wood, then tighten up well.

6 A circular seat of this type makes an attractive feature in its own right and even if infrequently used, it is worthwhile making it firm and level and giving it a new coat of preservative paint when necessary.

Potted herbs

At one time the only flowering plants seen in the cottage garden would have been herbs, or, loosely described, plants for a purpose; for medicinal use, personal or domestic hygiene or to add flavor to food. There was a vast range of these plants; although most have drifted back into the wild, others are the venerable predecessors of today's flower borders and many - in particular the culinary herbs - are enjoying an enthusiastic revival. Their appeal is multifaceted: they have beautiful and aromatic foliage to enhance the garden, properties to repel pests and protect other plants that are grown beside them, an irresistible attraction for bees and butterflies and they are essentially part of the lighter, healthier trend in cookery, with its emphasis on fresh vegetables and salads.

Some herbs are rampantly invasive and need to be sited very carefully away from the rest of the garden and out of the prevailing wind. Try containing them in pots on a bed of shingle, where the umpteen thousand seedlings can be easily hoed away. A basic collection of the most useful herbs would include parsley, thyme, sage, mint, bay, basil, marjoram, chives and fennel. Once you are acquainted with them, chervil, rosemary, tarragon, lovage and sorrel soon become 'must haves'.

Some herbs grown in containers will need to be renewed every two or three years. The woody ones, such as sage and rosemary, become sparse and leggy, while rampant spearmint and fennel get choked. However, marjoram, hyssop, sorrel, savory, tarragon and thyme, with their small roots and neat habit, will last for many years, just getting better.

Right: Potted lemon balm forms the center of this compact herb garden, which has been imaginatively planted as a patchwork in paving, where the herbs can be clipped and pinched to keep them in shape.

Flue liners are available in buff and terracotta, round or square.

1 *In an open-ended pot, the roots can grow into the earth beneath. At 9in(23cm) or 12in(30cm) in diameter, flue liners are large enough to accommodate the most vigorous species.*

2 *Settle the base into the ground and fill it two-thirds full with good-quality garden soil. It is not a good idea to use potting mixture.*

Above: *Quite apart from its value as a culinary herb, golden marjoram makes a superb pot plant, flowering in mauve or white and very attractive to bees. Also makes excellent ground cover.*

The flat-leaved parsley is a stronger plant with a better flavor than the curly-leaved variety.

If chives are left to dry out the plant will collapse. The flowers bloom in varying shades of lavender-pink in early summer and bees adore them.

The leaves of purple sage are as good in cooking as the common green one. It looks wonderful in the flower bed, with spikes of blue flowers in early summer.

Right: *Arrange the flue liners at varying heights, sinking some deeper into the ground than others. Put those herbs that enjoy moist conditions in the lower containers.*

3 *Place the plant in the flue liner and water it. Top up the soil until it is 2in(5cm) below the rim of the liner to retain moisture when watered.*

Thymus doerfleri 'Bressingham Pink'

51

Fruit without the fuss

Now that good fruit and vegetables are readily available all year round, people concentrate increasingly on cultivating flowering plants in ever smaller gardens without the space or need for a separate kitchen garden. You might suppose that growing fruit is no longer a practical proposition when you have to put up cages and protective netting, or the tree that shades your garden table attracts hordes of wasps as its crop ripens. However, there are ways of having fruit in the garden that are decorative and without the drawbacks. You might start with a fig tree that is suitable for growing outdoors. Unlikely as it may seem, it makes the perfect pot plant, as its roots need to be restricted to curtail its growth and produce more fruit. Over the past few years, strawberries have become popular container plants, even seen in hanging baskets. The perpetual varieties fruit in succession through the summer; remove any flowers that appear earlier to ensure a good crop. Alpine strawberries are charming at the edge of a cool border, 'Baron Solemacher' is an excellent choice, being without the runners that can otherwise be a nuisance. There are delicious soft fruit to use as climbers on walls or fences, thornless varieties of blackberry and loganberry being more compact and manageable than their prickly counterparts.

Right: The thornless logan-berry makes a good wall plant and fruits prolifically with little attention. Pick the fruit often and give a top dressing and feed in winter. The birds will take their share!

1 The little alpine strawberry 'Fraise du bois' makes a pretty plant for a pan or half-pot. First cover the drainage hole with a piece of broken clay pot.

2 Fill the pan up well with potting mixture so that there is plenty of depth for the roots and the plants will hang over the sides.

3 Make as deep a hole as possible, so that the long thin roots are not bundled up, and arrange the plant close to the side of the pot.

Growing a fig against a wall

1 This young fig tree, 'Brunswick', is growing in a 12in(30cm) pot against a sunny wall. Bury the pot so that the rim stands up 2in(5cm) above the soil level.

2 Water the pot in well; the rim will make watering easy. Every other year in winter, dig down and prune off any roots growing out of the drainage holes.

Above: A 'Brown Turkey' fig happily settled with white clematis 'Henryi' climbing through it. Do not feed for the first three or four years to keep the framework neat. Tie to wires 12in(30cm) apart.

Right: The thornless black-berry 'Oregon'. Hoe out any self-set seedlings immediately and remove fruiting canes to the ground straight after picking. Tie in new growth.

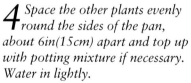

4 Space the other plants evenly round the sides of the pan, about 6in(15cm) apart and top up with potting mixture if necessary. Water in lightly.

5 Runners grow rapidly on this variety, so place the pot on a ledge or wall where they look attractive hanging down. Keep the container cool and not too dry.

Below: Rubus phoenicolasius, *the Japanese wineberry. It is important to remove the fruiting canes at ground level and secure young growth. Dress and feed in winter.*

These plantlets on runners can be used for propagation.

53

Flowering shrubs

Shrubs bring an established and rounded-out appearance to the garden, supplying substance, height, shape and texture; the muscle on the bones of the design. Needing little attention and producing dependable displays of often exquisitely scented blooms, flowering shrubs link and emphasize lawns and beds, providing the setting for other plants. The criticism that after flowering they are too dull for too long is addressed by lacing them with a climber for a second display. The perennial pea, *Lathyrus latifolia*, or *viticella* or *texensis* types of clematis are possible choices; because they need cutting down to the ground each year, they do not inhibit the shrub's own growth. Choose carefully, as shrubs are long-lived and usually exceed their given dimensions. For hot dry conditions consider *Buddleia nanho* or 'Pixie' forms, *Caryopteris*, *Cistus* (sun roses), hebe, lavender, *Perovskia* (Russian sage), *Santolina* (cotton lavender) or *Senecio*. These are all short, with greenish-gray or silver foliage, excellent grouped together, adding the beautiful foliage of the *Artemisia* for good measure. In normal conditions and sun or partial shade try *Ceratostigma*, *Chaenomeles*, *Deutzia*, *Hypericum*, *Potentilla*, *Spiraea* or *Weigela*, all of which are easy and trouble-free, of short to medium height. Find room for at least one or two of the magically scented *Philadelphus* and deciduous *Viburnum*, notably, V. *carlcephalum*, *juddii*, 'Aurora' or 'Diana', which all enjoy well-drained light shade. *Ceanothus* is for protected sunny sites, hydrangeas, magnolias and daphnes for slightly moist, protected shady ones; overall a treasury of riches to suit any situation.

Above: 'Belle Etoile' is one of the loveliest mock oranges, Philadelphus. *It is best planted among other shrubs or in a sheltered spot, where the unforgettable scent will be trapped to fill the garden.*

Left: The lovely color and informal habit of the Japanese quince, Chaenomeles 'Superba', lights up the spring garden. There are rose-pink, salmon and blood-red varieties. Do not keep it too dry.

Right: Magnolia stellata *is the daintiest of shrubs with clouds of starlike fragrant flowers. Shelter it from frost and morning sun in winter. It can be kept small in a container.*

Potentillas

The shrubby potentillas are a joy, with their easy-going habit and cheerful little flowers that reappear regularly from spring until the frosts. 'Abbotswood' is the best white, but there are yellow, orange, peach, pink and red varieties. Colors other than yellow or white will fade in hot direct sun and are hardy only in well-drained, but not totally dry, soil out of drying winds.

Above: Genista aetnensis, *the Mount Etna broom, eventually becomes a small tree, erupting in an airy golden explosion at midsummer. Like other brooms, it resents pruning of old wood.*

Right: Lavatera 'Barnsley', *the largest of the tree mallows, reaches 10ft(3m) in height and width. Smothered with red-centered white flowers fading to pink from midsummer until the frosts.*

Foliage texture

The texture of good foliage is an essential ingredient of the cottage garden as a stable and long-lasting counterpoint to the continually changing floral displays, because after their season of bloom, flowering shrubs tend to be uninspiring for the remainder of the year. To add interest and unify the garden, foliage shrubs are indispensable and adaptable, tolerating trimming and thinning as required. There are many beautiful colored forms, but use them sparingly, in separate areas, or the overall effect will be garish. The dogwood family, *Cornus*, produces some of the easiest and best foliage: green-and-white 'Sibirica Variegata', coloring richly in the fall, golden variegated 'Spaethii' and clear golden *C. alba* 'Aurea', which can stand full sun without scorching. For red accents look at forms of *Berberis*, such as 'Rose Glow' or 'Dart's Red Lady', or the superb, tall, purple *Cotinus* 'Grace'. Give them an open situation if possible where the sun will light them from behind. A small shrub with exceptional fall color is *Berberis* 'Kobold', which turns to flame and has neat green summer foliage. Bring silver into the garden with two *Elaeagnus*, 'Quicksilver' and *commutata*; both are very beautiful and grow to 10ft(3m). The latter's suckering stems will need cutting back periodically. Dense walls and blocks of foliage are not wanted, but a subtle interlacing of shapes and shades, each benefiting the others.

Below: Berberis 'Harlequin' has beautiful coppery, variegated cream, young foliage. It associates well with old roses, such as 'Irene Watts'.

Right: Neat and slow-growing, the corky winged stems of Euonymus alatus *are clothed in modest green leaves until fall, when each one turns a brilliant coral-red.*

Above: Golden hop, Humulus lupulus *'Aureus', is rough and slightly hairy to enable it to cling. It produces masses of hops when planted in a sunny site.*

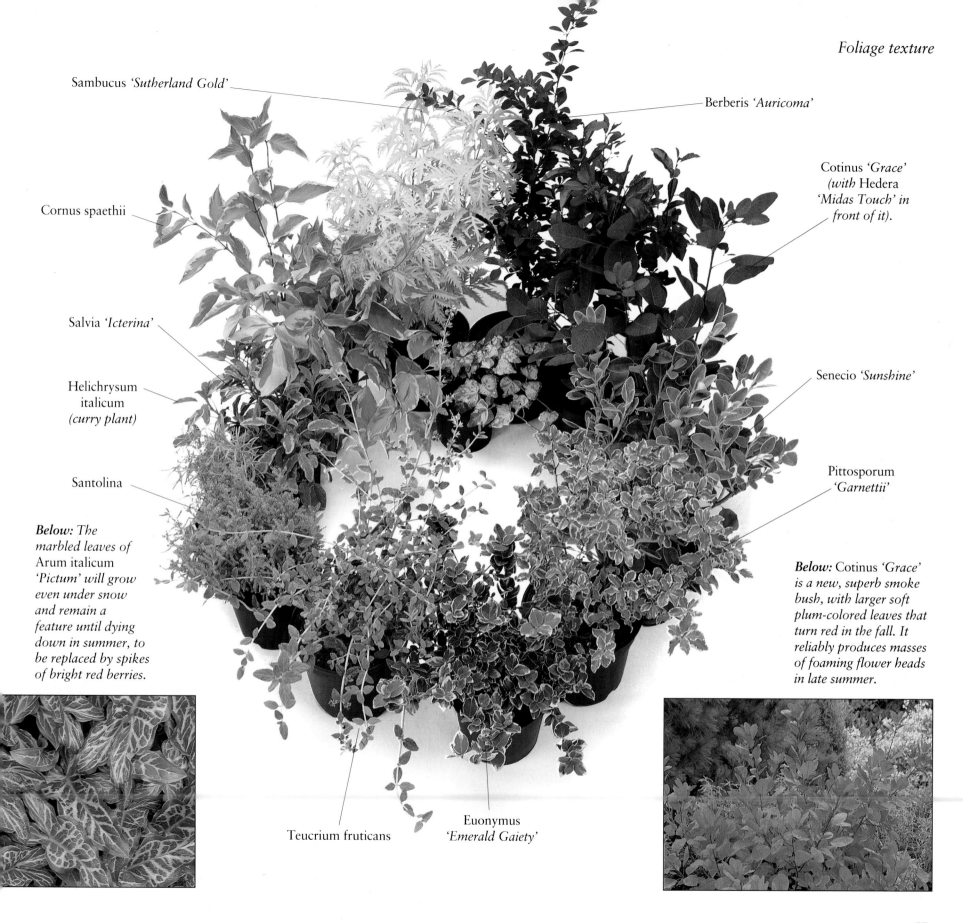

Sambucus 'Sutherland Gold'

Berberis 'Auricoma'

Cornus spaethii

Cotinus 'Grace' (with Hedera 'Midas Touch' in front of it).

Salvia 'Icterina'

Helichrysum italicum (curry plant)

Senecio 'Sunshine'

Santolina

Pittosporum 'Garnettii'

Below: *The marbled leaves of Arum italicum 'Pictum' will grow even under snow and remain a feature until dying down in summer, to be replaced by spikes of bright red berries.*

Below: Cotinus 'Grace' *is a new, superb smoke bush, with larger soft plum-colored leaves that turn red in the fall. It reliably produces masses of foaming flower heads in late summer.*

Teucrium fruticans

Euonymus 'Emerald Gaiety'

Clipping and shaping shrubs

Clipping and shaping some of your shrubs is not only practical but fun to do, adding interest and structure while restricting the subject to a limited space. Wall shrubs are particularly effective kept in soft informal shapes by pinching and pruning. This method can be used on almost any woody plant, from sage to pyracantha; prune to the desired overall outline and pinch out the growing tips regularly to promote compact bushy growth. Lavender, potentilla, berberis, rosemary and *Kerria variegata* will all make charming informal dwarf hedges to line paths or paving; shear them over lightly to keep them compact.

For short formal hedges, use dense small-leaved evergreens; box is perfection but extremely slow. Yew makes very hard wood and is difficult to keep small. With minuscule leaves in green, gold or silver-variegated forms, *Lonicera nitida* is fast and easy, satisfyingly quick to take shape, although less hardy and requiring frequent clipping.

A hedge should be broader at the base, to receive sufficient light and water, and taper towards the top so that severe weather does not split it open. You can convert large shrubs into delightful small 'trees' by reducing the stems to between one and three and removing all foliage up to shoulder height. Holly (*Ilex*), smoke bush (*Cotinus*), *Viburnum tinus* and *Elaeagnus* are all strong shrubs, able to stand on a single leg, but experiment to suit yourself. Shrubs grown as a color-associated group look attractive clipped in mounded outlines merging into one another, especially at a distance, to conceal a boundary fence. For example, *Forsythia*, golden privet, *Ligustrum ovalifolium* 'Aureum' and *Pyracantha* 'Soleil d'Or' at the back, with shorter *Lonicera* 'Baggesen's Gold', *Choisya* 'Sundance' and gold-variegated *Elaeagnus* in a staggered row in the middle and *Euonymus* 'Emerald 'n' Gold' and yellow-flowered *Potentilla* 'Elizabeth' in front.

Creating a standard holly

1 *'Moonlight Holly' is a female form of* Ilex aquifolium *'Flavescens'. Its leaves, especially when young, are flushed bright yellow, shading to gold.*

2 *To create a standard holly, choose a well-grown young shrub with a strong, straight stem. Snip off the side shoots with sharp secateurs.*

4 *When you have cleared enough of the stem, tie it to a cane in several places to support and straighten it while the standard is developing.*

5 *The side growths should be removed only below the cluster of horizontal shoots near the top of the leader. Shorten these shoots by half.*

Pruning pyracantha

To restrict the growth of vigorous pyracantha bushes without sacrificing the crops of brilliant berries, only cut young growth. The shrubs fruit on old wood, so by removing young shoots twice a year - once before flowering and again before the berries ripen, neither show is marred and shape is maintained. Besides the yellow 'Soleil d'Or', there are red and orange-fruited forms. Unpruned, Pyracantha *makes a fine shrub.*

Right: *The impressive wall of berries beside this doorway illustrates the success of this pruning technique.*

3 *Remove the side growth starting at the base, but take care not to cut too close to the main stem or you will weaken it for the future.*

6 *Remove any new growth that appears below the developing head. Pinch the tips of new shoots within the head at equal length. These initial stages are the same for any subject.*

Right: *A fine specimen of* Ilex *'Golden King', clipped in a striking double ball. As holly is very slow, this will have taken many years to reach its present size.*

Tree ivy as a shrub

Only the infantile growth of the common ivy is clinging and climbing. Deprived of support after a certain height, it ceases to cling and changes to the bushy flowering and fruiting habit of its mature form. A plant resulting from cuttings taken at this stage will bypass the infantile habit, producing the broad evergreen Hedera 'Arborescens'.

Right and below: Clipping this variegated form of H. 'Arborescens' promotes a compact habit and restricts the size.

Topiary for fun

Below: Using a garden snail as a model, this topiary one was shaped entirely by clipping and needed no training or tying-in. It is 39in(1m) high and wide after ten years and should be protected from icy blasts in winter. If you are choosing a fairly realistic animal shape and are doubtful about making a start, find a model to copy; children's toys and ornaments have the right stylized shapes. Rabbits, cats or ducks make good subjects as, in general, simple shapes are the most successful. Chunky globes, pyramids, eggs and cones that need no training or tying in are stylish and eye-catching, or try conifers trimmed in slender spires.

Topiary is purely for fun. There are preformed foliage shapes on sale and a variety of shaped frames to make life easier. However, these are both expensive and unnecessary; the whimsical result of combined predisposition of the plant and individuality of the topiarist is much more entertaining. Small-leaved evergreen shrubs create the most successful shapes, box, yew, privet and ivy being the most dependable. You can also modify an existing feature; an erect yew or juniper lends itself to binding and trimming to resemble the slender spire of a Mediterranean cypress, or a tall hedge to the introduction of windows. Parts of a shorter hedge could be allowed to grow up and then shaped. To start off a creature, tie canes in initially to hold the branches apart in the chosen direction until the wood has hardened. After that, frequent light clipping and judicious tying-in (not tightly) will thicken the subject up. If you make a mistake, wait for it to grow back in or modify the design - you make the rules! Little standard 'trees' of bay are well known; of ivy and honeysuckle less so, though they are equally appealing. Twist three good stems together and support them with a stake, continuing to twist them as they grow until they reach the desired height. Prune and pinch the tops as described on pages 58-59 to achieve a bushy globular head. Tender perennials have recently captured the public interest for container planting and some of these, such as the marguerites and heliotropes, make charming small standards for a pot.

This golden-leaved snail has been clipped from Lonicera nitida 'Baggesen's Gold'.

1 A variegated form of Lonicera nitida 'Silver Beauty' is going to be clipped as an 'egg' in a large pottery 'cup'. Select a good bushy specimen for topiary.

Binding and shaping

The 'Golden Irish Yew' and other erect, narrow conifers thicken with age or if their leaders are cut. Binding and clipping when they have achieved their adult height will maintain their youthful appearance.

Right: This grand old yew is one of a pair planted over 70 years ago. Yew is very slow-growing; a hedge needs only an annual pruning, but to keep topiary perfect, it will need cutting in late spring and the fall.

Below: Dwarf box hedges have been clipped for hundreds of years. The slowest variety, capable of growing only 15in(40cm), is Buxus sempervirens 'Suffruticosa'. Cut it twice a year to promote bushy growth.

1 Twist fine green garden wire round a stem in the base and wind it in a spiral up the tree to the top and down in the opposite direction, securing it at the bottom.

2 Bind it firmly but not too tightly, tucking in any large shoots that have escaped. Shear off any shoots that are growing out and that might spoil the shape.

2 This plant was roughly halved in height and left for six weeks to make more basal growth. Do the first shaping with secateurs.

3 At this stage it will not be possible to achieve much shape, but it is important to make certain that every tip is cut, starting with the longer ones.

4 Now that a dome shape has been roughly achieved, just clip and pinch as new growth appears. The egg will be complete in about two years.

The right rose

The cottage garden would not be complete without roses. Modern breeding has produced exquisite repeat flowering, disease-resistant hybrids in an astonishing range of colors. Inevitably this has been at the expense of the gentle grace and charm of the old roses, with their gloriously scented flowers in softer shades but only one flush of bloom. Nevertheless, a careful selection can exploit the virtues of both groups while avoiding the disadvantages. Hybrid Tea, or 'large-flowered', roses are out of place in the cottage garden, with the huge blooms and stiff ugly growth that result from the severe pruning they require.

Left: 'Graham Thomas' is one of the best of a beautiful new group called 'English Roses', with old-fashioned flowers and scent on low shrubs in a range of mouth-watering colors.

Pruning roses

Below: *It is important to deadhead repeat-flowering roses to bring them back into bud as soon as possible, rather than let them waste energy making hips.*

Above: *Cut at a leaf with a prominent bud in the axil where the stem is quite strong, perhaps as much as 12in(30cm) or so below the dead head to be removed.*

This exquisite little China rose 'Perle d'Or' has been in gardens for well over a hundred years. Its flexible stems grow to about 48in(120cm) with few thorns, flowering all summer and fall.

Left: *'New Dawn' was the first continuous-flowering rambler and is still one of the finest. Sweetly scented, reliable, healthy, and tolerant of hard pruning and any situation. Can be 10ft(3m) up to 25ft(7.5m).*

Above: *The lovely cerise flowers of 'Zéphirine Drouhin' have framed cottage doorways for over 125 years. It is completely thornless and blooms continuously with a delicious perfume.*

Flowering without a break the entire summer and fall, Rosa mutabilis has little pointed buds of flame-apricot, opens to honey gold and turns to tissue-paper rose before dropping. Needs a warm site.

The velvet flowers of the gentle climber 'Souvenir du Docteur Jamain' are so darkly red that they cannot tolerate direct sun. Perfumed, and with slender, flexible, practically thornless growth to 10ft(3m). Repeats well.

Above: *Rosa glauca (syn. rubrifolia) is of most value for its lovely foliage - a soft plum-gray like the bloom on a purple grape. It reaches 8ft(2.5m) with small pink flowers and good hips.*

The versatile clematis

There are varieties of clematis for every purpose: in sun or shade, to use as ground cover on banks or over tree stumps, through shrubs and into trees, or to blanket sheds and fences. The smallest can be kept in a pot, the most vigorous will drip delightfully off the eaves. Clematis support themselves by twining their leaf stalks around the nearest thing to hand - including their own stems - so the growing shoots need to be spread well out and tied in when grown on a trellis against a wall or fence. If this is not done while they are young, the stems will be impossible to separate, building up a choked mass of growth.

Although the sumptuous, large-flowered clematis are probably the ones that spring first to mind, in the cottage garden the more modest, but far easier and tougher types that flower on the current season's wood are worth their weight in gold, not only because they can be cut to the ground in winter, but also because they rarely succumb to clematis wilt. Neither do they resent the less hospitable conditions imposed by the demands of a tree or large shrub growing in close proximity.

The performance of the large-flowered clematis mirrors the care they receive, especially at planting time. Their roots must be kept cool in well-drained but not dried out soil, planted to a depth of 2in(5cm) above the root, with plenty of humus. They will not tolerate being cold and wet and windblown, or hot and dry and starved.

Clematis

Spring/Summer - no pruning
'Frances Rivis': blue-white alpine.
'Freda': cherry-edged-rose montana.
'H.F. Young': periwinkle blue.
'Marjorie': greeny peach double montana.
'Willy': Pale pink alpine.
Summer/Fall - hard pruning
'Perle d'Azur': sky blue.
'Prince Charles': silvery blue.
'Alba Luxurians': small, green-tipped white.
'Purpurea plena elegans': small double rose-purple.
Species - hard pruning
flammula: white, scented.
x jouiniana 'Praecox': ice-blue.

Above: In a sunny place, dainty spring-flowering C. macropetala fades to a delicate sky-blue. 'Maidwell Hall' is a good mid-blue, 'Markham's Pink' a dusky lilac-rose. Prune after flowering only to keep the plant tidy.

Left: 'Bill Mackenzie' is a superb form of C. orientalis, the orange-peel clematis, so-called because of the thick spongy texture of its 'petals'. Blooms from midsummer until the first frosts.

Right: *Viticella types of clematis are tough and reliable, with masses of flowers on new wood. 'Minuet' is distinctive, with its mauve or purple-edged white flowers held well above the foliage. The long stalks make it good for cutting.*

Below right: *Two of the best-known viticellas, 'Madame Julia Correvon' and 'Etoile Violette' scramble with honeysuckle through yellow roses on trellis.*

Above: *'Mrs. N. Thompson' is one of the most richly colored of the large-flowered clematis, with a glowing carmine bar on deep purple. Slow to get started; needs no pruning.*

Honeysuckles

The evocative scent of honeysuckle has typified the cottage garden for centuries; an easy climber that would scramble in from the hedgerow to twine itself round any available support. *Lonicera periclymenum*, the much-loved common honeysuckle, is one of a versatile race with scented flowers for every season, ranging from bushy shrubs to busy climbers covering huge areas. The climbers produce their distinctive whorls of flowers from early summer to fall, followed by clusters of juicy, bright, usually red berries. The majority require a cool, moist root run and semi-shade, but *L. etrusca* will romp happily to the roof or up a tree in full sun, while two very beautiful although unscented varieties, *L. tragophylla* and *L. tellmanniana*, will cope with complete shade. Bush honeysuckles include small, attractive evergreens excellent in garden situations.

Lonicera nitida is ideal for low hedges of 36-48in(90-120cm) or topiary. It includes a yellow form, 'Baggesen's Gold', which needs full sun, and the green-white variegated 'Silver Beauty'.

L. pileata is equally useful; tolerating heavy shade, its small, bright green leaves on horizontal growth are very effective as underplanting or coping with a difficult spot. Shrubby honeysuckles also provide the perfumed blooms of winter; *L. purpusii* 'Winter Beauty' and *L. standishii* being the most reliable and free. They produce sprigs of cream flowers from early winter to late spring on small to medium-sized bushes, followed by red berries in early summer.

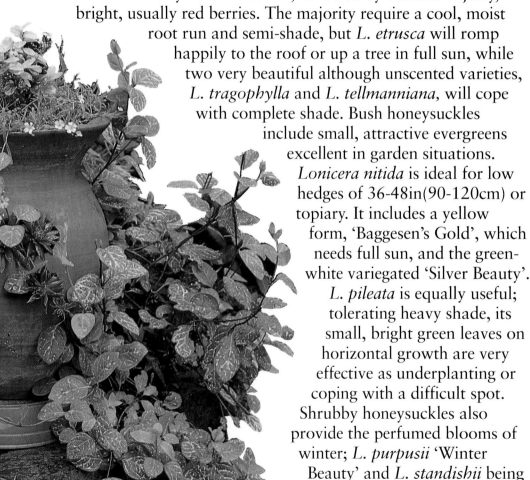

Above: The golden-orange flowers of L. tellmaniana are not scented, but make a superb display in a cool, shaded situation, out of cold winds.

Below: 'Graham Thomas' is vigorous and compact in growth, with masses of heavenly scented gold and cream flowers over a long period.

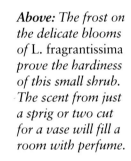

Above: *The frost on the delicate blooms of L. fragrantissima prove the hardiness of this small shrub. The scent from just a sprig or two cut for a vase will fill a room with perfume.*

Left: *The climbing Dutch honeysuckle 'Belgica' is shown here clipped and grown as a large bush. Flowering in early summer, it is followed almost immediately by the late Dutch 'Serotina'.*

Above: *With the deepest coloring of its group and good dark foliage, the ruby red and ivory flowered* Lonicera periclymenum *'Florida' is exquisite when grown with old roses.*

Essential perennials

With the landscaping, trees and shrubs in place and beds prepared, it is tremendously exciting to reach the stage of choosing the flowers for your garden. A cottage garden is composed of many different plants growing closely together, rather than large drifts of a few types. While annuals lend themselves to a kaleidoscopic riot of color, perennials are better used in harmony to make the garden feel restful and more spacious and to create different moods. Most perennials die back to the rootstock in winter and put out new leaves every spring. Some are very long lived, increasing in size until a deteriorating flower display signals the need for division. The larger perennials are the mainstay of bed or border, flowering at the same time each year, a keystone to anchor and add substance to the scheme of an associated group of plants. With close planting, it helps to use varied height and habit; loosely categorized, classic garden plants are grouped as described in the panel. Study the result of your planting while it is in bloom and make notes of any rearrangements needed in the fall; you may think you will remember but you won't! Do not hesitate to move or dispose of plants; experience is only gained by trial and error.

Above: This pretty Sidalcea *'Elsie Heugh' is like a miniature hollyhock growing to 3-4ft(90-120cm). It blooms through summer to early fall.*

Plant groups

Erect spikes: Aconitum, *some* Campanula, Delphinium, Iris, Kniphofia, Lupin, Lythrum, Penstemon, Salvia, Sidalcea, Verbascum, Veronica.

Clustered heads: Achillea, Astrantia, *some* Campanula, Centranthus, Lychnis, Phlox, Sedum.

Mound forming: Alchemilla, *some* Aster, Centaurea, Dianthus, Erigeron, Geranium, Geum, Gypsophila, Heuchera, Hosta, Mimulus, Nepeta, Potentilla.

Clump forming: Anthemis, Aquilegia, Aster, Astilbe, Dendranthema, Doronicum, Gaillardia, Helenium, Helleborus, Monarda, Paeonia, Papaver orientale, Scabious, Solidago, Tradescantia, Trollius.

Right: The lovely Rosa *'Excelsa', grown as a standard, is the keystone of this glorious bed. It is echoed in red lychnis, contrasted to limpid yellow oenothera and blue veronica, and softened by notes of pink from phlox and astilbe.*

Right: These hardworking plants look after themselves until the fall. Salvia, rose and chrysanthemum are laced together by poppies and potentillas, with kniphofia to add height and structure.

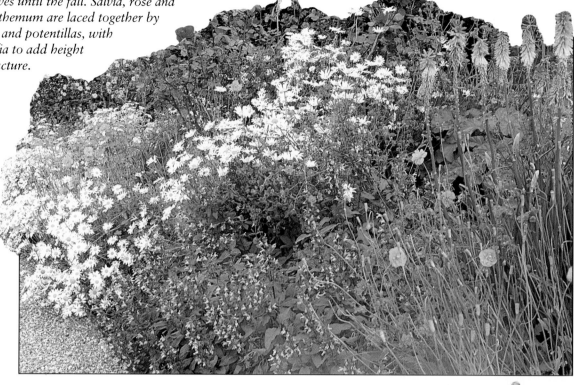

Above: 'Bleeding Heart', 'Dutchman's Breeches' and 'Lady's Locket' are all common names of Dicentra spectabilis. Keep it cool and out of the wind.

Left: Penstemon 'Garnet' is one of the finest perennials, making masses of spikes of elegant tubular flowers from summer onwards. Adored by bees and reliably hardy.

Right: Delphinium 'Peace' is one of the belladonna varieties, which are a better choice for the cottage garden than the huge Pacific hybrids. With their more slender, branching habit, they need no staking to provide a stunning display.

Beautiful biennials

A small group of plants falls between the annual and perennial categories; biennials are hardy, grown from seed sown in early summer, taking the remainder of the year to develop sufficiently to flower the following season. The flowered plant then dies away, often leaving seedlings to repeat the cycle. Some of the best-loved cottage garden flowers are in this group; although *Alcea*, the hollyhock, is actually perennial, it is so rust-prone that it is better treated as a biennial. There are no problems with *Digitalis*, the foxgloves. They seed around, but are enchanting anywhere and flower for a long time if deadheaded.

Forget-me-nots and spring are automatically associated, their clouds of tiny azure flowers a perfect accompaniment to any other spring blooms, such as *Lunaria* (honesty). Although usually seen with pinky purple flowers, honesty also has a rarer white form, 'Stella', with beautiful white-variegated leaves. 'Sweet Williams' belong to the *Dianthus* family. Their fragrant, spiky-looking eyed flowers are borne in chunky velvet clusters in mixed shades of pink, white and red, distinctive in the summer border.

Two other sweetly perfumed old world beauties are the richly vibrant wallflowers for spring, equally at home in beds or containers, and Brompton stocks for summer. They have exquisite velvety colors set off by felted gray foliage, but sadly are also much loved by slugs. Uniquely, *Campanula pyramidalis*, the chimney bellflower, is delicately scented. It throws up tall, thin stems studded with clear blue or white bells for many weeks during the summer and fall.

Propagating zonal pelargoniums

The essential cottage pot plant known as 'geranium', in reality the zonal pelargonium, is usually treated as a biennial, cuttings being rooted in the fall for the following year. However, they are prone to rot and a safer method is to take them from an overwintered parent plant, cut back by half in the fall, repotted and kept without watering in a cool place where there is not the slightest risk of frost, until it starts into growth in spring, when you can take your cuttings.

Right: Alcea rosea, *the true cottage garden hollyhock, is prettier in its simplicity than the double ones. There is also a good clear yellow, and* A. nigra, *an almost black-red.*

Below: The digitalis species are becoming more popular, not as top-heavy as the cultivars, and more reliable. D. mertonensis *is a lovely apricot and* D. grandiflora *a clear pale yellow.*

Planting a barrel with biennials

1 Drill a drainage hole in the base of a halved distillery barrel. Line it with plastic, pushing a bit through the hole and snipping it off.

2 Cover the hole with a crock so that it does not get clogged and fill the barrel with potting mixture to 2in(5cm) below the top.

3 Level the compost surface and trim off the surplus plastic evenly, turning the cut edges over and tucking them down inside.

4 Space the Myosotis (forget-me-not) seedlings around the edge, keeping 8-9in(20-23cm) between them, and plant them in evenly.

5 Plant the Cheiranthus cheiri (wallflower) seedlings in the center of the barrel, filling up with extra potting mixture if needed. Water in. Use a proprietary plant food according to the instructions.

Above: The golden-yellow, fringed tulip 'Maja' looks stunning in a bed of Myosotis that picks up the blue of the painted wall boards above it.

Below: Cheiranthus cheiri spreads its fragrance from late spring to early summer. The smaller orange or yellow C. allionii continues through summer.

71

Summer and late-season bulbs

Because almost all bulbous and tuberous plants have narrow bladelike leaves, they contrast well with clump-forming plants and can make plenty of impact in a small space. Although the majority bloom from winter to late spring, there are enough important categories to maintain an unbroken succession all year round; for example, varieties of *Allium,* members of the onion family, will cover four months from late spring and are as pleasing dried, as when in bloom. In early summer the ancient Madonna lily, *Lilium candidum,* will fill the garden with its scent from a sunny sheltered spot. It is followed a month later by the exquisitely elegant *Lilium regale,* a quintessential addition to the cottage garden, and *Lilium martagon,* with its many-branched heads of tiny purple turks caps. These three species, unlike most lilies, are lime-tolerant and easy to grow.

Galtonia candicans, the summer hyacinth, stands impressively at over 39in(1m) in a sunny border in midsummer, while the modern hybrids of *Crocosmia* - notably 'Star of the East' (amber), 'Jenny Bloom' (soft yellow), 'Rowallane Yellow' (golden), 'Spitfire' (fiery orange) and 'Vulcan' (flame-orange) - produce their flowers from mid- to late summer, accompanied by the rainbow colors of the hybrid gladioli, although the latter are more suitable for formal bedding schemes. The smaller, less rigid species gladioli look better in the cottage garden.

Agapanthus, gorgeous in multi-blues or white, brings substance and quality to the late summer display until everything turns pink for the remainder of the year, with the slender wands of the angel's fishing rod, *Dierama pulcherrimum,* followed first by drifts of *Cyclamen hederifolium* and then by delicate spring-blossom-pink *Nerine,* ending well into the frosts with the satiny red or pink cups of *Schizostylis.*

Below: *These elegant nerines need the protection of a warm wall, sharp drainage and shallow planting if they are to thrive. The neck of the bulb should stand above soil level.*

Right: A. rosenbachianum, *here dramatically outlined against a mass of blue ceanothus, is one of the best alliums, reliably blooming on strong stems at 2ft(60cm) in early summer.*

Left: *The ivy-leaved cyclamen is an amazingly tough and engaging little flower, increasing rapidly when undisturbed in a cool dry site. Do not plant deeply.*

Planting crocus

All crocus and colchicums grow well in containers, but are best naturalized in grass, where they can multiply undisturbed. Mow around them until the foliage has died down. Unlike the colchicums, Crocus speciosus is a true crocus that flowers in the fall, a fine free-flowering blue that readily increases.

The flowering shoot is a minuscule protruding tip.

A small dimple with a dark core indicates the root area of the corm.

1 *A terracotta pan or half-pot makes an ideal container for small bulbs. Start by placing a piece of broken pot over the drainage hole.*

2 *The corms need to be well-drained, so put a layer of grit in the base before half-filling the pan with potting mix. Smooth it down.*

Colchicum 'Beaconsfield' - mistakenly called 'Autumn Crocus'.

3 *Carefully position the corms about an inch apart, making sure that they are the right way up. If in doubt lay them on their sides.*

4 *This 9in(23cm) diameter pan takes 20 corms, spaced evenly over the surface of the potting mix. They are about 2in(5cm) below the rim.*

5 *Cover with potting mix almost to the rim. Smooth down gently but firmly and finish with a sprinkling of grit. Water lightly.*

Scents in the garden

For the cottage gardener, it is possibly the scented plants that, above all, evoke the mood, of aromatic foliage every bit as much as blossom. Flowers release their scent at different times of day and in varying conditions. Consider the heavenly perfume of mock orange (*Philadelphus coronarius*) on a hot afternoon, the mingled delight of the white-flowered tobacco plant *(Nicotiana alata)*, night-scented stocks *(Matthiola bicornis)* and honeysuckle *(Lonicera periclymenum)* at dusk; or maybe the heady fragrance of sweetbriar foliage *(Rosa eglantine)* filling the garden after rain. The *Dianthus* family includes many favorites, such as sweet Williams and the old-fashioned pinks and carnations. *Phlox* and stocks are sweetly and subtly scented, while lilies are best placed at some distance, as they are almost literally a knock-out! On a warm summer's day, the delicate fragrance of sweet peas will drift to blend with *Campanula pyramidalis* and *Primula florindae*. Narcissi, lily-of-the-valley and wallflowers are among the earliest fragrant flowers of the year, with *Primula auricula*, which deserves a raised bed in order not to miss its gorgeous scent. Lilac is beautiful but brief in early summer, with pungent hawthorn and elderflower - disliked by some! Lavender, jasmine and honeysuckle have been perfuming cottage gardens for centuries, together with the much-loved old roses. The leaves of lemon verbena *(Lippia citriodora)* are intensely lemon-scented, equalled by the spicy aroma given off by the foliage of *Halimocistus* in a sunny spot.

Above: Grow lilac, Syringa vulgaris, such as this single white 'Madame Florent Stepman', on its own roots, rather than grafted stock, to prevent suckering and promote bushy compact growth.

Left: Daphne odora produces rose-tinted waxy flower clusters with exquisite fragrance in late winter. Needs a protected site. The gold-edged Daphne 'Aureomarginata' is a hardier variety.

Left: The cool elegance of the lily-of-the-valley, Convallaria majalis, *belies its toughness; it will break up tarmac when in the cool shaded position it prefers, with ample moisture at the root.*

Philadelphus

There are dozens of the beautiful white-flowered mock oranges to choose from. Some with pink-blotched and single flowers, others pure white and fully double. However, it is the least glamorous species, Philadelphus coronarius, *and its golden and variegated forms that are the most entrancingly fragrant. They are happy in light, dry shade, so you can plant one in among your more showy shrubs to trap in that enticing scent.*

Left: *Billowing masses of rambling rose 'Sanders White' provide a gorgeous backdrop to this curving path lined with lavender, which will release its volatile scent at the slightest touch.*

Below: *Not all forms of the sweet pea,* Lathyrus, *are scented. Many of the modern dwarf strains and exotically flowered ones, as well as all the perennial types, are not. Nevertheless, the old perennial pea* Lathyrus grandiflorus *in two-tone magenta pink is a prolifically flowered early climber well worth seeking out.*

Right: *The sumptuous beauty of the many-petalled rose 'Charles de Mills' is equalled by its glorious perfume. A very old rose, it grows into a manageable bush at 4ft(120cm) high and wide.*

Attracting bees and butterflies

The essential sound of summer in the cottage garden arrives with the bees, drawn by a selection of the plants to which they are irresistibly attracted. These include all the scented flowers, even when pungent rather than sweet, as in the members of the onion family, and hawthorn blossom and elderflower. Scabious are also among their favorites, especially the giant 6ft(2m) yellow form *Cephalaria*, which reduces bees to such a stupor of delight that they can be seen laid out sleeping on the flowers through a warm summer night. They also spend hours patiently moving in and out of foxgloves and other tubular flowers, such as penstemons; even being too small to enter does not lessen the appeal of this type of flower, as the continual activity on sage and catmint *(Nepeta)* proves. If you are lucky enough to have a lime tree nearby, the humming of the bees at flowering time resembles the sound of distant traffic, under the spell of the glorious perfume. The hundreds of different species of bees that visit garden flowers each have their particular favorites, so the more diverse the planting, the greater the invitation to all the insects - in particular the hoverflies and ladybirds that play such a vital role in the garden's defenses against aphid attack.

Beautiful buddleia

Everyone knows about buddleia and butterflies - a bush in bloom is never without a cluster of butterflies dividing their attention between the 'butterfly bush' and the large, late-flowering sedums. The most numerous are the small tortoiseshell, peacock and red admiral, with a few commas and painted ladies and an occasional hummingbird hawkmoth.

Plant this intensely blue Salvia ambigens in gritty soil in full sun and give it a protective winter dressing of bark or leaf mold in winter.

Penstemon 'Garnet' is a vigorous, beautiful plant that flowers all summer. It is one of the hardier penstemons, as shown by its relatively narrow leaves. Very similar to 'Ruby'.

Origanum 'Purple Charm' is one of the more showy and ornamental forms of the herb marjoram. They have attractive clustered flowers on wiry stems in shades of mauve-pink to purple.

Verbena bonariensis will survive only very mild winters, but given a hot, gritty site, it will leave seedlings behind for the following summer.

Pink Lythrum 'Rosenaule' *is a loosestrife and like all other members of its family prefers a dampish site in sun, but will also tolerate normal border conditions.*

Pot marjoram, a well-known culinary herb, also makes neat and reliable ground cover. There is a pretty golden-leaved form with white flowers.

Allium pyrenaicum is one of the last members of the onion family to bloom. Its neatly clumped, straplike leaves are semi-evergreen and make a good edging to paths or paving.

Below: *Bees will doze all day on the flowers of any of the alliums. Chives are one of the earliest to bloom, their flowers then fading from bright purple to pale pink. Cut back hard after flowering to encourage growth.*

Above: *The buddleia flowering season coincides with the appearance of several of the best-known butterflies. They sate themselves on the sweetly scented blooms.*

Hardworking cranesbills

There are some families of plants that are a staple of the cottage garden, and the cranesbills, or hardy geraniums, are one of these; it would be difficult to have too many. They are in no way similar or related to zonal pelargoniums, commonly but mistakenly called 'geraniums'. As ground cover they are unequalled, the majority of their hundreds of varieties making soft leafy mounds of varying size from diminutive alpine forms for growing in paving, to strong plants for the border or to mass beneath trees. The colors possess a magic of their own in their ability to blend and contrast effortlessly with the old garden plants. Luminous purples, magentas, cerises, blues, pinks and whites glow from softly textured green, occasionally gray, foliage, making the geraniums excellent companions for old roses, or a foil for purple and silver leaves.

Divided, lobed, deeply or finely cut, the appeal of the geraniums lies as much with the foliage as with their flowers. Some are evergreen, some aromatic and some have attractively shaded markings, or color well in the fall. Cutting early-flowering types back hard in midsummer will produce a further flush and strong new growth, keeping the plant healthy and tidy until the end of the season. Other varieties produce their flowers on ever-lengthening trailing stems throughout the summer and fall until the frosts. Let them fling these 'arms' to good effect over low shrubs or mound up around a pot. These good-natured plants combine a long-lasting display with an ease of cultivation and maintenance that makes them indispensable to the modern garden.

Above: *'Johnson's Blue' is one of the most popular and easy geraniums. It has a long flowering season from midsummer to fall and grows happily in sun or shade.*

Above: *The double form of the Himalayan geranium known as 'Birch Double' is a smaller plant than its parent, making a spreading mat 12in(30cm) high. Cut it back after flowering to produce a second show.*

Left: *Put Geranium psilostemon beside a rose and its long trailing stems of intense magenta flowers will climb all summer through the thorny framework.*

Right: *'Russell Prichard', an old and well-known hybrid with a low neat habit, is an ideal edging plant for paths or paving. Divide it regularly.*

Left: Geranium macrorrhizum 'Album' makes superb ground cover. It blooms in early summer with prettily pink-stemmed white flowers and aromatic leaves that color well in the fall on the pink form 'Ingwersen's Variety'.

Below: This little alpine, G. 'Ballerina', blooms all summer without a break on neat tufts of gray-green leaves. Put it in paving where it can be seen.

79

Stitching the garden together

Even when everything is in place and the planting is complete, you are going to find odd gaps and difficult corners, a lanky plant or a clematis with browning lower leaves (all do). Then there is the hole that appears in your beautiful association of plants when a major contributor fades, or slugs demolish it before it is even allowed to contribute. At the other end of the scale are the 'special' plants, pampered and cossetted, that stand out looking smug and artificial. Remember that 'cottage' planting should look as relaxed and natural as possible and that in the wild the soil is always clothed, so you need to find plants of a modest nature that can be used in quantity without being overpowering, to provide a background and stitch the garden together. Small-scale plants of mounding, running or trailing habit that are cut back or removed after flowering are ideal. In spring, use forget-me-not *(Myosotis)* to create a blue haze linking plants and bulbs, and little bronze-purple *Viola labradorica* to run busily about covered with mauve violets. Let *Viola cornuta* weave through cool beds in summer, the frothing lime flowers of *Alchemilla mollis* billow softly around larger plants and shrubs. Underplant roses with *Nepeta* x *faassenii* or carpet a hot bed with *Anthemis cretica*, the filigree silver-leaved marguerite. Look for plants to suit your own needs that can be used a lot or a little, moved about or thrown out, without being really noticeable.

Above: As the pink rockery phlox fades, the self-set white or lilac-flowered seedlings of Viola cornuta *fill the space and bloom all summer.*

Right: Heartsease rapidly fills any space left by larger plants. Its little 'faces' appear in a variable mixture of yellow, mauve and purple.

Left: Allium albopilosum *is better grown among shorter plants, its unattractive foliage smothered and concealed here by the small white marguerite and lilac-blue geranium.*

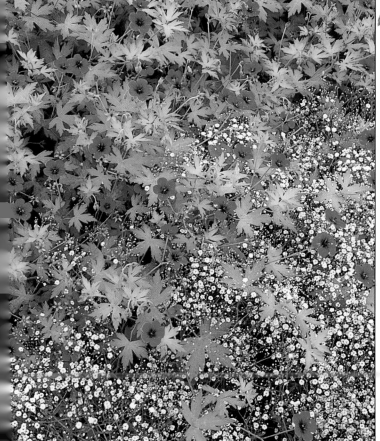

Above: Taller Allium aflatuense *also 'borrows' foliage and substance from the strong clumps of* Persicaria 'Superbum' *and* Alchemilla mollis *that perfectly stitch up the edge of this border.*

Left: From early summer to late fall, Geranium 'Ann Folkard', the star of border seamstresses, sends out 6ft(2m) trails of black-eyed magenta flowers from slender clumps of gold-green leaves.

Right: Alchemilla mollis is equally effective whether massed by itself or used in any color combination. Cut hard back in midsummer, it will produce fresh new growth.

Below: You can enjoy the silken beauty of the Iceland poppy, Papaver nudicaule, *indoors, as it makes a good cut flower. Technically a perennial, it is shortlived and better treated as a biennial (see page 70-71).*

Poppies everywhere

Poppies are irresistible and perfect for the cottage garden. They seed themselves everywhere and can be difficult to dislodge, but earn instant forgiveness with their joyous riot of color. The first to bloom is *Meconopsis cambrica*, the perennial Welsh poppy, with its clear yellow or orange flowers. There are breathtaking blue forms of *Meconopsis*, but these difficult acid-lovers are not reliably hardy. 'Californian poppies' belong to the *Eschscholzia* family and are the easiest possible hardy annuals. The petals form satin cups of brilliant yellow or orange, or pink, red and cream in the newer cultivars. Once grown they seed around forever, though easily removed where not wanted. Shirley poppies are the colored forms of *Papaver rhoeas*, the wild red field poppy; graceful plants with clouds of fluttering flowers like tissue paper butterflies in gorgeous shades of pearl to old rose. The purity of color of the shining silken petals of Iceland poppy, *P. nudicaule*, has to be seen to be believed. It is a temperamental biennial of flawless beauty, but worth every effort. With fully double heads of light red shredded petals, 'Fireball' is a miniature form of the large perennial oriental poppy, which mixes well with the annuals. So, too, does another perennial, *Papaver heldreichii*, with neat, flat rosettes of foliage and soft orange, tissue-thin flowers on slender wiry stems. It is worth seeking out. Last and most profligate, the opium poppy, *P. somniferum*, adds its slightly sinister mauves and purple-reds, sometimes double and fringed, contrasted by blue-gray leaves.

Right: The earliest to bloom is neat little Meconopsis cambrica, *the Welsh poppy, happy in damp shady crevices or under hedges. The flowers appear on and off throughout the year. There is also a pretty double form.*

Right: Shirley poppies appear reliably year after year, self-set in the position where the seed was first sown. They are lovely, carrying themselves at a useful 30in (75cm). A large color range has been developed, including mother-of-pearl shades of soft grays and pinks and mixed-color doubles.

Above: It is easy to see why this form of the field poppy, P. rhoeas, is called 'Ladybird'. It has seeded prolifically into this potato patch, but being shallow-rooted is easy to remove.

Right: Californian poppies flower until the frosts cut them down. A dry hot bed suits them very well and they associate brilliantly with all the blue-flowered plants happy in the same situation, such as veronica, salvia, cornflower, lavender, globe thistle, sea holly and caryopteris.

Easy annuals

Working downwards from the largest and most permanent features of the garden to the most fleeting, ends with the annuals; plants with an entire life cycle encompassed by half a year. From seed sown in spring, rapid growth produces a mass of flower and therefore quantities of seed to secure the next generation, exhausting itself by the fall. There are two distinctly different ways of using annuals. Those that are not hardy in cold spring weather need to be propagated under glass or bought as seedlings for planting out after the frosts. Petunias, pelargoniums, ageratum and verbenas are among the plants that fall into this category, and are used chiefly for bedding or container growing. Hardy annuals are wonderful for creating the carefree, exuberant mix of bloom and color that characterizes the cottage garden. Much of the seed they cast will survive the winter, and offspring will appear the following year in the most unlikely places with a spontaneity that is impossible to contrive. Most annuals are unscented, but there are a few treasured exceptions, such as stocks (*Matthiola* and *Malcolmia*) and mignonette (*Reseda*). Neither of these has a significant flower, but the half-hardy tobacco plants (*Nicotiana alata*) and *Heliotrope* 'Cherry Pie' are both beautiful and fragrant, as are blue petunias and the older climbing sweet peas. Keeping a space for hardy annuals with their short lifespan provides the opportunity for changing the effect every year. The following are some cottage garden classics: corncockle, cornflower, cosmos, flax, larkspur, love-in-a-mist, marigold, nasturtium, scabious and the giant sunflower.

Above: Traditional giant sunflowers on 10ft(3m) stems are too unwieldy in modern gardens. Cultivars such as 'Incredible' are a more manageable 39in(1m). Finches enjoy the seeds.

Above: Try mixing the glowing colored petals of marigold, nasturtium, day lilies, chives and viola in with a salad. Make rose petal sandwiches or float borage flowers in a summer wine cup.

Right: Iberis (annual candytuft) mixed with Nigella (love-in-a-mist) - still better in its original blue than mixed shades. Dry the fascinating Nigella seedheads for winter decoration.

A random scatter

For an explosion of summer color, mix together the seeds of a collection of annuals for sowing in one place.

Add the seeds to sand to bulk them up so that you can spread them more finely.

Californian poppy (Eschscholzia)

Red flax (Linum grandiflorum)

Shirley poppy (Papaver rhoeas)

Marigold (Calendula)

Larkspur (Delphinium ajacis)

Cornflower (Centaura cyanus)

Above: The sand marks where you have scattered the seed. To prolong the display, make two sowings four weeks apart, pricking out the weaker seedlings growing too close together.

Above: Flower heads on hybrid verbenas such as 'Linda' are arranged as little 'posies'. Their free-flowering, bushy habit makes them ideal edging plants for a summer border.

Right: The brilliant shades of pot marigold, mixed blue and purple cornflowers and rose-red Godetia stand out in front of a band of sky-blue Nigella. They will self seed.

Fruits of autumn

A lavish display of fall color and fruits makes this the favorite season for many gardeners. In the cottage garden, hips, haws, berries and crab apples are greedily plundered by the garden birds, but some varieties hang on the branches into winter. Crab apples abound in yellow, amber, pink, orange and red - and for rowanberries, add white to this range. The evergreen pyracanthas are abundantly covered with red, orange, golden or yellow berries if not clipped - but the birds love them in all their colors and a blackbird will eat 30 at a time. Cobnuts, hazlenuts and filberts make a good, large cottage garden hedge, although you may not see many nuts if there are squirrels in your neighborhood. Hawthorn haws are particularly sought by pigeons, which become remarkably enterprising in their efforts to move among the dense thorny twigs, developing a type of 'wing' walking. Some of the roses - notably the *moyesii* and *rugosa* varieties - have enormous and exotic hips that last well into winter. A shrub with stunning color-combination seed capsules is *Euonymus*, either *E. sachalinensis* or *E. europaeus*. The shocking-pink seed capsules open to reveal the bright orange berries within. These look even better after the brilliant, red fall foliage has dropped. A climbing relative, *Celastrus orbiculatus*, has a similar, though more modest, display of tawny yellow and orange berries. On a less acid to neutral soil, deciduous *Callicarpa* has clusters of small berries in similar colors that stay on the bare branches after the brilliant fall-tinted leaves have come down. Set a dish of the green-gold 'quinces' of the *Chaenomeles* on your table to capture their elusive and magical perfume.

Above: The hazlenut, Corylus avellana, *forms a thicket of tall stems if you do not remove the suckers annually. It makes an excellent wild hedge, smothered with long golden lambs tails in spring.*

Left: Only gardeners on acid soil can enjoy the marble-like berries of Gaultheria mucronata, *which last through the winter. The bushes are evergreen, fruiting in colors from white to crimson and purple.*

Below: *An enticing selection of blackberries, damsons, crabs, sloes, hips, haws and elderberries. To make hedgerow jelly, gently simmer 4lbs of fruit to 1 pint of water until soft. Strain through a jelly bag without squeezing, add 1lb sugar per 1 pint of juice and boil until the setting point is reached. Eat with meat or on toast.*

Right: *No cottage garden should be without a crab apple, with its prolific crops of little rosy or golden apples. Malus prunifolia var. rinki is a small tree with pretty almond-pink spring blossom.*

Above: *Deciduous Euonymus sachalinensis blazes with fall color when the leaves turn and the branches are strung with long-stalked clusters of rosy seed capsules.*

Below: *Rugosa roses are distinctive for their bright green, dense foliage, which turns to gold and russet in the fall, and huge, polished, flattened round hips. Can make large shrubs.*

87

Winter beauty

Above: *The profuse display of elegant flowers on* Viburnum bodnantense *'Dawn' makes an arresting sight in the winter months.*

Below: *The fragrant straplike flowers of* Hamamelis mollis *'Pallida' appear on bare wood after its radiant yellow autumn foliage has dropped.*

Winter is a season of surprises in the cottage garden, even apart from the decorative value of its foliage and seed heads. Many of the flowering shrubs coming into bloom are among the most sweetly scented of any. The wintersweet, *Chimonanthus praecox*, an otherwise unremarkable bush, opens heavily fragrant small purple and yellow bells, on a plant that reaches 10ft(3m) against a sunny wall. Give *Garrya elliptica* wall protection, too, as the evergreen leaves are susceptible to wind burn. The male variety, 'James Roof', drips with silky silver-green tassels up to 16in(40cm) long.

Although unscented, the starry yellow flowers of winter jasmine, *Jasminum nudiflorum*, cover every inch of the bare twiggy stems like a blaze of sunshine; but it requires tying in to a support and frequent clipping to give of its best. A dark, but not too heavily shaded, corner would make the perfect setting for a witch hazel, *Hamamelis*, to show up the delicate tufts of fragrant yellow or orange flowers strung along the bare, spreading branches. An alternative selection for the same situation might be *Mahonia* 'Winter Sun', with sprays of scented yellow flowers and handsome evergreen foliage.

From leaf-fall to bud-burst, perfumed pink flower clusters emerge on the old wood of *Viburnum bodnantense* 'Dawn', in company with the paler pink blossom of *Prunus subhirtella* 'Autumnalis' and the exotically fragrant white-flowered shrubby honeysuckle 'Winter Beauty'. Even without benefit of flowers or foliage, the indispensable dogwoods, *Cornus*, present brilliant displays of vivid red or yellow young stems, providing they are cut to the ground every other year in late spring. As a good small hedge for shade the dwarf evergreen shrub, *Sarcococca humilis*, emits an amazing fragrance from tiny almost invisible winter flowers. And for unequalled winter ground cover, the glossy green summer leaves of elephant-ear, *Bergenia purpurea*, turn a brilliant ruby-red.

Above: Chimonanthus praecox *may be no great beauty, but its fragrance is sublime. For best results, plant it in full sun in poor soil in a spot sheltered from frost and icy winds.*

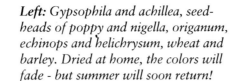

Left: Gypsophila and achillea, seed-heads of poppy and nigella, origanum, echinops and helichrysum, wheat and barley. Dried at home, the colors will fade - but summer will soon return!

Right: If protected from bitter frosts, winter jasmine puts out its cheerful little flowers from late fall to spring. Needs training up. Reaches 10ft(3m) against a wall.

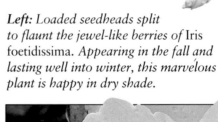

Left: Loaded seedheads split to flaunt the jewel-like berries of Iris foetidissima. Appearing in the fall and lasting well into winter, this marvelous plant is happy in dry shade.

Below: Once established, do not disturb Helleborus niger or it may never bloom again. H. orientalis, the Lenten rose, is less temperamental.

Index to Plants

Page numbers in **bold** indicate major text references. Page numbers in *italics* indicate captions and annotations to photographs. Other text entries are shown in normal type.

Credits

The majority of the photographs featured in this book have been taken by Neil Sutherland and are © Colour Library Books. The publishers wish to thank the following photographers for providing additional photographs, credited here by page number and position on the page, i.e. (B)Bottom, (T)Top, (C)Center, (BL)Bottom left, etc.

Glyn Barney (© Colour Library Books): 35(TL), 61(TR)
Gillian Beckett: 47(BR)
Eric Crichton: 13(BL,CB), 15(BC,BR), 20-21(B), 24(BL,TR), 25(BL), 32(L), 33(L,TR,BR), 43(BR), 45(BR), 52(TR), 53(TR,BR), 55(L), 56(BR), 59(CB), 63(TR), 66(L,TR,BR), 68(B), 69(TR,BR), 79(TL,BL), 81(BR), 82(BR), 83(TL,BR), 86(TR), 87(BR), 88(BR)
John Feltwell/Garden Matters: 42(BC), 68(TR), 71(TR), 77(CBR)
John Glover: Half title, 12(TR,BR), 13(BR), 15(TL), 19(TR), 32(BR), 34(TL,CB), 35(TR), 38(TC), 39(TL), 40(BL), 41(TL,TR,BC), 42(TR), 43(T), 48(BR), 54(TR), 56(BC), 57(BL,BR), 59(TR), 61(CR), 62(BL), 63(TL,BR), 65(BR), 67(TL,BL), 69(TL), 70(TR,BR), 73(TL), 74(BL,TR,BR), 75(T,BL,BR), 77(CTR), 78(TR), 79(BR), 80(B), 81(BL), 85(BR), 86(B), 87(TL)
S. & O. Mathews: 19(BR), 25(BR), 44(TC), 44(CBR), 82(L)
Natural Image: 78(BL), 80(TR)
Clive Nichols: Copyright page (Graham Strong), 10, 13(TR), 14(T)Designer Julian Dowle, 15(TR), 29(TR), 35(BL), 40(BR), 43(BL), 46(BL), 50(TR), 51(TL), 54(BL,BR), 55(R), 56(TR), 64(B,TR), 65(TR), 67(R), 71(BR), 72(R), 73(TR,BR), 78(BC)Designer Sue Berger, 81(TR), 84(TR), Designer Julie Toll, 85(C), 87(TR), 88(TL), 89(TR,BL,BR)
Photos Horticultural: 83(TR)
Derek St. Romaine: 38(TR), 53(CR), 65(L), 84(BL), 84-85(B), 87(L)
Tim Sandall: 39(TR), 69(BL), 81(TL)
Harry Smith Horticultural Photographic Collection: 42(BR)

Author's acknowledgments

Thanks are due to Blooms of Bressingham for generously loaning the plants, especially Tony Fry and Anne Etherington for their patient response to my questions. Claudia Williamson for her expertise and willing commitment to the typing. Shelley and Jonathan Choat for the provision of studio facilities. Anne and Alan Round, Margaret Horbury and Rose Mayhew for the kind use of their gardens. Floods Climbers for the unstinting supply of stock plants. Paigles Flower Shop for the dried flowers, and Jan Nawrot for saving the day. The publishers would also like to thank Garboldisham Garden Center and T. H. Waters for supplying seats and pots used for practical photography.